The Limits of
Organizational Change

HERBERT KAUFMAN

THE UNIVERSITY OF ALABAMA PRESS
University, Alabama

CONTENTS

ACKNOWLEDGMENTS

I SHOULD LIKE TO THANK ROBERT B. HIGHSAW AND COLE-
MAN B. RANSONE for the invitation to take part in the lecture series of the Southern Regional Training Program,
for their gracious hospitality, and for their counsel.

I am also indebted to the following members of the
Governmental Studies community of the Brookings In-
stitution for their critiques and suggestions: Michael J.
Couzens, Thomas E. Cronin, Leonard Goodwin, Albert Z.
Guttenberg, William R. Keech, Craig Liske, Donald R.
Matthews, Daniel A. Mazmanian, Bruce Oppenheimer,
Allen Schick, David Seidman, Da·id T. Stanley, Gilbert Y.
Steiner, James L. Sundquist, John Wanat.

In addition, I am deeply grateful to the members of the
staff and the student body of the University of Alabama
who attended the lectures and by their questions and
comments prompted much further thought and revision.

The Brookings Institution was most generous in releas-
ing some of my time for the preparation, delivery, and
revision of the lectures. I profoundly appreciate Brookings'
contribution to this enterprise.

Finally, my thanks to Mrs. Robert Reinhart, who typed
and retyped the manuscript with unfailing good cheer.

INTRODUCTION

FOR ABOUT A QUARTER OF A CENTURY, I have been an organization watcher. I watch mostly large organizations, and mostly in the public sector, but they all fascinate me. It isn't a secret vice; I do it in public much of the time. I can't break myself of the habit.

It's an easy habit to get into. At the beginning, I was drawn to the practice casually by treatises purporting to set forth principles and "laws" of large-scale organization. The world was complex, confusing, and disorderly, and I was strongly attracted by the promise of a rational interpretation and a scientific body of knowledge. Later, I was impressed by the common features of the organizations I worked in; so much of the experience gained in one seemed applicable to all the others. My original motivation was reinforced.

Unfortunately, my hopes and expectations were a little premature, to say the least. Under the probing analysis of thoughtful critics, the principles evaporated and the laws disappeared. Early "scientific" treatises turned out to be prescriptions for administrative success without much in

1

the way of evidence as underpinning, and some of them were revealed to be so self-contradictory as to border on the meaningless.

That's when I started to watch in earnest. Since the classical literature was not much help, I thought it would be instructive simply to observe in order to find out what does actually go on in organizations.

The more I watched, the more confused I became. I would clutch at a generalization only to find it honored more in the breach than in the observance. I found that the features common to numbers of organizations cloaked myriad differences. The symmetry of hierarchy gave way to the anarchy of bureaucratic infighting. Formal models failed to fit reality. But I kept on watching and hoping and waiting.

It seems to me that the study of organizations and of organization theory is making progress, and it is not unreasonable to hope for significant advances in the near future. Meanwhile, however, the invitation to offer these lectures provided me with an incentive to canvass my own impressions to see what I could make of all these years of both systematic and haphazard observation. Without striving for methodological rigor or logical elegance, I have tried to record in an orderly way a distillation of the most general of those impressions. This is not a comprehensive survey of literature or an effort to describe the state of our knowledge. Rather, it is a very personal understanding of some aspects of organizational life and behavior that seem to me important.

A summing up obviously does not break new ground. But a compact statement of this sort may suggest some associations among elements of organizational behavior simply because so many things do get juxtaposed that would be more widely separated and submerged in larger treatments. At the very least, I trust it will serve as a convenient summary of factors in organizational change and stability that students will find useful—as a point of departure or a whipping boy.

A good many key terms are only loosely defined. Whenever I tried to make them precise, I bogged down in a semantic quagmire. Ultimately, I comforted myself with the hope that their meaning would be made clear by their context—the last defense of ambiguity. One colleague characterized the result for the reader as comparable to picking up wet watermelon seeds from a slippery table. On the other hand, his spirited critique suggested that we were engaged with each other even if we were not in agreement. Sacrificing extensive definition may sometimes aid clarity by permitting the argument that frames the concepts to unfold fully and quickly.

Thus, for example, although the discussion centers on organizational stability and change, it nowhere specifies whether it refers primarily to procedure or structure or input and output. I believe it applies with equal validity of all of these. Some of the illustrations are therefore chosen from one of these possibilities, some from the others, some from combinations. This makes for a certain degree of untidiness and elusiveness, and may render the argument more vulnerable to attack than a more restricted claim might. Going off the deep end, however, is a useful art at times, even when the dive is not so clean as it might be. It seemed to me more was to be gained by the risk than by efforts at caution and exactness.

Similarly, some illustrations come from the experience of bureaus, some from departments, some from governments as a whole, and some from societies considered as organizations. Again, the result is distressing to anyone who demands rigor and precision. Under these conditions, a reference to "internal" and "external" can be confusing, and a constituent element can "change" while the more inclusive organization containing it remains "essentially the same." Again, however, I think that the meaning is clearer in context than it could be made by formal definition at the outset, and that the reader can make the transition from one level of abstraction to another without losing his way. Moreover, since I decided to take the plunge and contend that the analysis applies to *all* large organizations, it was not unjustifiable to reach for examples wherever I could find them.

I proceeded with the faith that these admitted weaknesses would not be fatal. If the burden of the book has substantive merits, then the defects of inadequate formal definition and insufficient specificity could be remedied later on; better to get on with the first approximation now. If it is fatally wrong at its conceptual core, then it could not be saved merely by elaborating the glossary. Admittedly, I have chosen a course easier for me than for the careful reader. On the other hand, the resulting product is mercifully brief.

Why, however, should anyone bother with a volume which the author himself confesses is neither novel nor analytically elegant? The only reason I can think of is that the line of argument, whether right or wrong, may stimulate readers to better formulations of their own (which, incidentally, I trust will eventually help me to correct *my* errors) ; setting down on paper what is often merely taken for granted sometimes has this effect. If the book does nothing more than this, it will, in my mind, have justified the effort of writing it. If it achieves anything more, I will be especially gratified—and will vehemently deny any feelings of surprise.

CHAPTER 1

WHY ORGANIZATIONS
TEND NOT TO CHANGE

ORGANIZATIONAL MORTALITY AND CHANGE

ORGANIZATIONS apparently die in great numbers. Admittedly, to define organizational death is not a simple matter (see Appendix). Nor do we have more than fragmentary and uncertain evidence about the mortality rate of organizations. Still, the impressions of thoughtful observers and such partial indicators as we have all seem to point toward a large death rate. Chester Barnard, for example, was not resorting to pure hyperbole when he declared that

> successful cooperation in or by formal organizations is the abnormal, not the normal, condition. What are observed from day to day are the successful survivors among innumerable failures. . . . [M]ost cooperation fails in the attempt, or dies in infancy, or is short-lived. . . . Failure to cooperate, failure of cooperation, failure of organization, disorganization, disintegration, destruction of organization—and reorganization—are characteristic facts of human history.[1]

Such data as we have on survival in the business world buttress this assertion. With a population of about four million business concerns in the United States, something approaching four hundred thousand of them have been discontinued annually in recent years. Many more tens of thousands disappear as a result of acquisition by other firms or mergers or the like. At the same time, more firms commence operations each year than are discontinued. Without more information, we cannot be sure of all the implications of these figures. Nevertheless, they suggest very strongly that the turnover among business organizations is very high.[2] If other kinds of organizations have corresponding experience, conditions that would be considered epidemic for complex biological organisms seem to be the norm for human collectivities.

This state of affairs is in some respects precisely the opposite of what we might expect. Biological organisms, after all, have many fixed and (up to now) unalterable traits; no matter how clever they become, no matter how ingenious they are at compensating for the limitations imposed by their fixed characteristics, they cannot escape them. In a dynamic world, it is understandable that these might in time prove lethal.

Biological organisms also have limited life spans. Sooner or later, excepting perhaps some species that reproduce exclusively by fission, they all must die.

Taking both factors into account, large numbers of deaths among complex biological organisms are to be anticipated.

Human organizations, on the other hand, are not self-evidently locked into particular characteristics as fixedly as organisms are by their respective genetic heritages. Theoretically, armed with all the knowledge and wisdom they can mobilize, they should be able to modify themselves, structurally and behaviorally, as a swiftly changing environment requires, and thus continue indefinitely once they have been started.

Moreover, they are not burdened, as far as we can tell, with fixed life spans. To be sure, why the life spans of organisms are limited, and why each species has its own distinctive limit, is still something of a mystery. Like organizations, organisms are open systems that continuously replace their constituent elements as these elements are used up or cast off. There are no universally accepted explanations of why the process, once begun, stops. That it should stop in human organizations, which enjoy so much freedom and discretion in the choice and deployment and use of materiel and personnel, is even more puzzling.

Yet organizations do cease to exist, and apparently in droves. Their rate of cessation probably equals or exceeds the death rates of human beings, at least in the industrialized parts of the world.

I do not propose to offer a comprehensive explanation of this curious set of circumstances. The causes of organizational death are doubtless too numerous and complicated to be treated briefly. All I shall do is indicate why it is that organizations, which presumably labor under fewer built-in constraints on structure and action than most organisms, are often in fact far less capable of changing than the presumption implies. In view of the fact that we live in a constantly changing world, it is reasonable to infer that the limitations on organizational change are contributing factors in the demise of some organizations. The discontinuation of organizations for this reason, even though it is not the only cause or even the most common one, has implications for organization theory; I shall explore these in the closing section of the book.

Let me emphasize that I am not contending that organizations must change continuously or die. It is conceivable (and perhaps probable, if the record of biological species is at all applicable) that an organization comes to occupy relatively a stable ecological niche in which it can survive and flourish for long periods without altering its structure or practice in any significant way. When this happens, change could be harmful and even fatal.

Nor do I intend to imply that change in organizations always conduces to the introduction of a new order. One can imagine, and doubtless find in history, cases in which immense inventiveness and resourcefulness were employed to preserve the status quo. Old orders may be maintained as well as transformed by originality and innovativeness.

In short, I am not saying that organizational change is invariably good or bad, progressive or conservative, beneficial or injurious. It may run either way in any given instance. But it is always confronted by strong forces holding it in check and sharply circumscribing the capacity of organizations to react to new conditions—sometimes with grave results. To seek the lessons in those forces and their consequences is the object of this little volume.

BARRIERS TO CHANGE

The causes of failure to change the behavior and/or structure of organizations when such rigidity turns out to be disadvantageous or even fatal can be grouped in three broad categories: acknowledged collective benefits of stability, calculated opposition to change, and inability to change. Let us look at each of them in turn.

COLLECTIVE BENEFITS OF STABILITY

Life in groups, especially in groups engaged in cooperative undertakings, is inconceivable without regularities of behavior, which is to say repetitive behavior. No group can stay together without such regularities; the absence of such regularities (if such a state can be imagined) would be the ultimate in disorganization. To live in association with other creatures thus requires acceptance of constraints.

Yet people apparently prefer living in groups to any imagined alternatives. Why? Some theorists answer in terms of rationality—the computation of the benefits of social living as contrasted with life in isolation, the blessings of security and enrichment one enjoys as consequence of cooperating with others. Some theorists explain this preference in terms of mankind's social nature, which is to say the inseparability of human characteristics and achievements from the societies in which humans are nurtured. The theorists who rely on rationality to account for the formation of collectivities believe that individuals would *choose* to live together even if they could live apart. The others deny that human beings could live completely apart and still be human; they really do not have that choice. Whatever it is that brings and holds people together, however, all theorists agree that living together requires a great deal of regularized behavior. Social critics may object to a particular *pattern* of regularities, or to the ways the regularities are maintained. But even the most ardent individualists accept the need for regularities of some kind as a condition of human life.

At the organizational (as compared with the societal) level, this implicit understanding is the justification for routines, standard operating procedures, prescribed behaviors, and mandatory ways of communicating. If anyone would change them, the burden of proof is normally on him.[3] What exists may have its defects, but disruption of the ongoing regularities could be even worse. Collective wisdom favors the status quo. Since *some* regularities are needed, and all required regularities have unpleasant features, why risk known imperfections for unknown ones? Why gamble an established imperfect order for possible disorder? The logic of collective life thus has a conservative thrust; it lends authority to the system as it stands. Even disadvantaged members of organizations or societies ordinarily acquiesce grudgingly in the systems that treat them badly; "all experience hath shown," says the Declaration of Independence, "that mankind are more disposed to suffer, while evils are sufferable, than to right themselves by abolishing the forms to which they are accustomed." Moreover, it is easier to do nothing than to do something, and inaction sustains prevailing arrangements. The respectability of familiar institutions sanctioned by time, the ordinary distaste for "chaos," and the strategic advantages of the defenders of what already obtains aid the consensus on the need for stability to keep organizations from introducing changes which postmortems inform us they should have adopted.

CALCULATED OPPOSITION TO CHANGE

Over and above this general predisposition against change in the social climate of most organizations, specific proposals for change are almost sure to encounter vigorous obstacles in the form of organized resistance from individuals and groups both inside and outside. Some resisters will be intent on protecting advantages they derive from things as they stand. Some will be agitated about the possible erosion of standards of quality in goods and services they treasure. Some will resent having to bear the costs of change.

Prevailing advantage. Without claiming there is a fixed fund of organizational benefits such that any increase in benefits for some participants inevitably reduces the benefits for others, we may safely assume that it is a rare change (or one of negligible proportions) which does not affect someone adversely in some respect, at least as he sees his interests. Most people who perceive adverse effects on them and who link them, rightly or wrongly, with a proposed change can usually be counted on to resist as mightily as they can. I do not deny that there are altruistic people who readily surrender advantages they possess in order to benefit those less fortunate. In most cases, though, the advocate of innovation is well advised to prepare for opposition. In fact, people sometimes seem to resist innovations even when they cannot identify any results harmful to them, simply because they grow anxious about consequences they cannot foresee that *might* injure their interests. Occasionally they resist even when they *know* they will suffer no injury in order to exact concessions or other advantages in return for their acquiescence.

The range of rewards that induce people to contribute to organizations is so broad and intricate that it is virtually impossible to design any change that avoids reducing some of them. To compute just the material rewards of employment is difficult when, in addition to pay, working conditions, convenience of work-site location, leave and retirement policies, insurance plans, and other such considerations are taken into account. And when intangibles are considered, the only thing one can be quite sure of is that some people will feel threatened and deprived by any change. Status, influence, fame, ideology, compassion, security, pride, fear, hatred, loyalty, moral obligation, intellectual challenge, love, and every other sentiment known to mankind play their roles. Job title, job classification, physical location, reputation of product or unit, race or nationality or religion of coworkers, for example, may influence as profoundly as salary a given person's individual decision to contribute to an organization or to sever relations with it. Similarly, customers and investors and suppliers and lenders may be as much influenced by consideration of an organization's hiring policies, or its efforts on behalf of pollution control, or its race relations practices, or its overseas branch locations as they are by pricing or interest or dividends records. Seldom, therefore, does any change avoid impinging negatively on some interests.

In addition, strategic position and access often provoke opposition to a change even when no direct payoff or loss follows. Thus, bureau chiefs commonly resent reorganizations that put new administrative levels between them and their department heads. Interest groups inveigh against changes that disrupt the relationships they have established with the old structure. Professional associations try to restrict practice of particular trades, or appearances before tribunals, to their own members, and often seek to confine qualifications for specific offices to their own ranks. Not all innovations affect strategic relations, but any that do will most assuredly provoke strenuous resistance on the part of those who see themselves disadvantaged by proposed changes, even if the impact is not immediate or concrete.

Protection of quality. Changes in organizational structure or behavior may be opposed on the ground that they would impair the quality of goods or services rendered. Some of the resistance to open enrollment and to elimination of grading in universities, for example, was based, rightly or wrongly, on the conviction that the outcome would compromise advanced education and lower the average of student performance. The opposition of the medical profession, rightly or wrongly, to practitioners of the "naturopathic" healing arts is unquestionably stimulated by concern for safeguarding the public as well as by anxiety about potential competitors. The reluctance of judges to let the accused in criminal cases present their defenses themselves instead of through lawyers is motivated at least as much by considerations of justice and maintenance of the integrity of the judicial process as by any wish to protect the monopoly of the legal profession on representation in courts. To distinguish between self-interested and public-interested action is extremely difficult, but in seeking the origins of opposition to change only the most cynical would automatically dismiss all motives other than personal or group advantage.

Psychic costs of change. The advocates of change naturally concentrate so heavily on the benefits to be derived from their recommendations that they sometimes lose sight of the personal effort and agony of people who have to accommodate to the new patterns. Over and above the advantages lost and the penalties inflicted by opponents, beyond the humiliation of becoming a raw novice at a new trade after having been a master craftsman at an old one, and in addition to the expense of retraining and retooling, is the deep crisis caused by the need to suppress ancient prejudices, to put aside the comfort of the familiar, to relinquish the security of what one knows well. Put aside the social and financial incentives to stand fast; they are treated in other parts of this discussion. After those are excluded, it is still hard for most of us to alter our ways. The psychic costs of change can be very high, and therefore go into the balance sheet on the side of keeping things as they are.

In addition, the psychic risks of pressing for an innovation are substantial. If the change is adopted and fails, the embarrassment and loss of stature and influence can be chilling to contemplate; the costs and benefits of the old ways are at least known. If battle is joined on behalf of change, the proponents are likely to be belabored from all sides—often by people who never thought about the issue before. Some critics will accuse the advocates of being too timid in the struggle, while others will portray the campaign as evidence of hunger for power; some will call them tools of vested interests while others depict them as running amuck; some will complain of the innovators' readiness to experiment wildly at the expense of those they serve while others ridicule them for unwillingness to try anything more daring than marginal adjustments. To win allies, the proposed reforms must be amended and weakened and compromised until the expenditure of effort seems hardly worthwhile. Meanwhile, the drama of the struggle often arouses expectations among the beneficiaries out of all proportion to the realities of the improvement; instead of winning applause and gratitude, the innovators often reap denunciations from those they thought they were helping as well as from their adversaries in the controversy. And anyone with any experience in such contests is aware that he may end up with obligations to supporters whose purposes he does not share, and with fleeting credit but lasting enmities.[4] On balance, then, the members or other contributors to any organization are presented with much stronger incentives to act warily than daringly. Precedent serves as a valuable guide because it clearly defines the safe path; in a minefield, wise men step exactly in the footprints of predecessors who have successfully traversed the hazardous area.

The collective benefits of stability and the calculated opposition to change thus weigh heavily against innovation even when the dangers of inflexibility mount. Even more massive hurdles, however, are raised by two sets of factors that prevent change rather than merely discourage it. Let us call one set mental blinders, the other systemic obstacles to change.

INABILITY TO CHANGE: MENTAL BLINDERS

Programmed behavior. In all social groupings, regularities of behavior essential to collective life and enterprise are programed into the members of the groupings by the groupings. That is not to say that every organization or society employs precisely the same programming methods. Some, for example, rely heavily on family instruction or tribal indoctrination, others on specialized instructional corps (teachers, training officers), still others on apprenticeship techniques, and a few on police and thought control. In every case, since much of the programming takes place by imitation and observation and other informal means, a good deal of it is inadvertent, and may occasionally run counter to what the leaders would prescribe if they could. A great deal of programming, however, is deliberate, particularly in organizations of great complexity.

Some social scientists believe there are fundamental behavioral programs common to all social groupings that must be instilled in all members. At a high level of generality, the proposition seems to be true. In specific organizations, however, what is impressive is the special twist given behavioral regularities adapted to the particular circumstances of the individual case.

The behavioral programs of participants in complex organizations are usually specified in great detail as a result of intensive division of labor. Every component must perform according to specifications or else there is a danger that the entire operation will be disrupted. People are therefore screened and groomed for the positions they will occupy, especially if the positions provide opportunities for the exercise of discretion. Incumbents are "fitted" into the ongoing system. In spite of criticisms, the process continues, probably even in the organizations to which the critics themselves belong. The imperatives of complex organization make it seem inescapable.

Procedures for filling positions are the hinge-pins of the process. Potential candidates are screened not only for skills and aptitudes, but for attitudes and even for personality traits. (An incidental consequence is the development of intensive specialization in personnel screening, both inside and outside the employing organizations; the professional interests of personnel specialists reinforce the intrinsic job pressures to fit people to organizational needs.) As the criteria of selection and advancement become known, schools and universities tend to adapt their curricula to those requirements in order to provide precisely the kinds of candidates sought, and training institutes spring up to prepare applicants for very specific openings. The initial steps in socializing people to the norms of their employers are thus taken long before the candidates are inducted into their organizations. Implantation of suitable outlooks and styles, as well as of needed technical backgrounds, begins very early. And since the focus is always on the organization as it currently stands, present actual needs taking precedence over future possible ones, the whole system is geared to keeping things as they are.

Important as the preservice and selection processes are in producing personnel with the appropriate predispositions and abilities, it is *within* the organizations that the fitting of the individual to the requirements of the system takes on particular intensity. The organizations proceed methodically to try to shape the values and perceptions of new members, and to instruct them in what they must do if they would like to get ahead. The initial match of candidate to system is at best a rough approximation; the fine adjustments take place later on.

The methods are well known and need not be treated here in detail.[5] "Misfits" are weeded out at the end of probationary periods. Personnel are systematically rotated to broaden their perspectives, deepen their understanding of the problems of their colleagues (and thus make them more tolerant of difficulties that would otherwise infuriate them), intensify their loyalties to the organization as a whole, and draw them into the social as well as the work structure of their peers. Promotions identify the attributes prized by the leaders and advance people who fit the organization's requirements; they signal to everyone what the preferred behavior patterns are. Where "career service" obtains, with higher positions filled exclusively (or even primarily) by advancement from below, new leaders are especially likely to have been in the system long enough to have internalized its folkways, objectives, procedures, and outlooks. Advisers are chosen for their sympathy with the viewpoints of their executives;

while no wise administrator surrounds himself with sycophants or seeks unanimous counsel, neither does he bring in people whose ideology is at war with his own.

At the same time, most large organizations conduct training programs. Some of them are for purposes of indoctrination, and are so labeled. But even when they are of a more technical nature, they involve instruction in the values of the organization as well as in its way of doing things.

Many organizations also encourage and support symbolic activities intended to strengthen the solidarity of their memberships. Country clubs, athletic teams, social gatherings, and house organs, for example, help build identification of officers and employees not only with each other but with the organization as such.

And the job itself gradually becomes a way of life for many organization members. They learn the manual, master the methods, and forge understandings with their fellows until the whole system becomes second nature to them. Directives, orders, commands, instructions, inspections, audits, reports, and all the other means of organizational control, however irksome they may once have been, are gradually accepted as one's own premises of thought and action, until compliance with them is no longer reluctant, or even indifferent, obedience but an expression of personal preference and will.

Tunnel vision. The problems that absorb a person day by day take on an importance in his scale of values quite at variance with the value systems of most people outside his limited ambience. That may be why the adjective "petty" is so often associated with bureaucrats. Bureaucrats appear to set such store by triumphs that seem rather trivial when measured against the standards of outsiders, to get so exercised about minor deviations from prescribed procedure, and to be so punctilious about matters of slight consequence to anyone whose perspectives are not identically circumscribed, that they sometimes impress one as making a fetish of trifles.

To the extent these impressions are accurate, the behavior they describe develops not because the members of large organizations are so different from the rest of us, but because they are so like everyone else. To everyone, objects close by look larger than objects far off; small hills in the foreground appear greater than mountains in the distance. Therefore, if we dwell among small hills that obscure mountains from view, the small hills will often play the parts of mountains in our lives. And when we speak of a man's having perspective on a problem, we mean that he views it from a standpoint which permits him to distinguish hillocks from mountains.

In large organizations, division of work into tasks of diminutive dimensions is coupled with intensive specialization that locks many members into the continuous performance of only one or a few such tasks. Hillocks loom disproportionately large in the perceptions of people whose horizons are cramped in this way. Few of us can escape comparable distortions under such circumstances.

So clerks who work on forms all day become adept at detecting every error and may grow stubbornly insistent on complete accuracy in execution of the blanks. Meticulous observance of the rules takes on the character of a cult. Small symbols of status are objects of ardent quests. Office gossip is assiduously sought. Unions engage in work-stopping jurisdictional struggles over the exclusive right to perform activities of negligible importance. In all such cases, the people involved are likely to argue that they are

defending a perimeter of "vital principle." To an independent observer, they appear to be so engrossed in
their small tasks that they have forgotten how small the
tasks are, and to be at the same time so bored with repeti-
tion that obduracy about details furnishes welcome relief
from the relentless, unending routine.

To people in this position, the attempts of innovators
and reformers to introduce change—even modest, incremental adjustments, as the reformers see them—therefore stand forth as highly disruptive and threatening, and
become calls to battle. Insularity reinforces inflexibility.

Indeed, insularity not only endows small features of
their little world with overwhelming salience to bureaucrats but also renders them less aware of and sensitive to
currents of change in the larger environment that reduce
their traditional operations to anachronisms. For example,
extraordinary efforts—in some cases by civilians—were
required to convert some navies from coal to oil for fuel,
and later to persuade them of the practicality of nuclear
propulsion. Both admirals and generals at first denied the
full significance of air power, as the ordeal of General
"Billy" Mitchell dramatically attests. A high-ranking officer detailed to modernize the United States Post Office in
New Deal days was reported to have quipped about the
methods then in use: "It is not true that they were still
using quill pens when I arrived—but there were feathers
on the floor!" Henry Ford clung obdurately to production
of his successful Model T while his competitors ate into
his market by catering to changing customer tastes and by
taking advantage of new mechanical developments.

If tunnel vision and the consequent inflexibility of specialists commonly impede perception of opportunities for
technological improvement, which are comparatively easy

to discern and evaluate, imagine how much more inhibitory these factors are when less tangible changes are involved. Colonial offices of imperial governments blithely persisted in their established ways while whirlwinds of nationalism gathered and engulfed them. Modern management techniques and analysis were ignored and resisted in many companies and government agencies for years. Teaching methods admirably suited to the urban clientele and the state of knowledge in earlier generations persisted long after both had changed and the effectiveness of education in cities had declined. Distribution of public services in familiar patterns grinds on while excluded or inadequately served segments of the populace, once quiescent and resignedly despairing, mobilize to articulate and if necessary to enforce their demands for more equitable treatment.

Organization leaders and members who seem to be unaware of transformations that are conspicuous to other observers are not wanting in intelligence, humanity, and good intentions. They slip into their unyielding ruts by imperceptible stages because their attention is so totally concentrated on the specialized functions that must be completed day by day if the output of their organizations is not to cease altogether.

"Brave New World?" After some years of all these pressures, both unconscious and deliberate, an organization's policies and procedures are apt to become for many people, including (indeed, perhaps especially) those at high levels, the natural, automatic ways of acting. Not only are they *disturbed* by suggestions that change is required; they are *astounded* because any other pattern is unimaginable.

Having said all this, let me retreat a bit and admit that

I have exaggerated for the sake of argument. In fact there are limits to human tolerance, and there are some controls and demands that no amount of brainwashing can make acceptable. The most totalitarian regimes have not succeeded in achieving the degree of mental manipulation portrayed in *Brave New World* or *1984,* and there is hyperbole even in *The Organization Man.*[6] Every complex organization, with its large numbers of specialties and separate trades and geographical dispersion and administrative echelons, encompasses so many different perspectives and interests that it is impossible to suppress new ideas entirely. Cross-cultural contacts in the modern world of swift travel and communication cannot be prevented. Industrial societies nourish such a profusion of organizations that most people are members of at least several of them, and the competition for loyalties, obedience, and contributions precludes any single world-view from obliterating all others. Furthermore, science and technology generate diversities and heterodoxies. Fortunately, the dictator's vision of a populace unable to think an unapproved thought is still beyond the capacity of any man or clique.

All the same, tendencies in this direction are found in all large-scale organizations. If the tendencies are never totally fulfilled, the effects of their partial fulfillment are nonetheless significant. Even competing interests work out mutual accommodations that reinforce prevailing arrangements; trade unions, for example, buttress conservative impulses by insisting on seniority as the main grounds for advancement. This depersonalization of promotional standards undoubtedly does vanquish management strategies for rewarding docile rather than challenging workers, but it also assures the advancement of people on whom the mechanisms of conformity have had the longest time to work. Discount by half the effectiveness of the mechanisms I have just described, and the impediments to innovative thinking are still impressive. They reduce the likelihood that new goals or methods will be conceived by people in such organizations. They curtail the probabilities that such proposals will be adopted even when they are put forth. And they diminish the capacity of members to alter their own behavior even when they see the advantages of the proposed transformations. In short, these mechanisms lock people and organizations into present patterns.

Inability to Change: Systemic Obstacles

Mental blinders are obstacles to change that function "inside" people. To be sure, many of the "internal" controls on the thinking and behavior of all of us come from "outside"; by learning and conditioning, we make them part of ourselves. Nevertheless, even when new ideas surmount such obstacles, they encounter barriers built into the system itself rather than into the individuals making up the system.

Resource limitations. For example, some organizations would eagerly change their structure and behavior but for the fact that change of this kind often demands resources they are unable to mobilize.

Like the mice that knew exactly what to do to reduce their vulnerability to the cat, the leaders and members of organizations sometimes cannot do what they agree must be done for their collective benefit. The goal may be to modernize a primitive economy, or to update an enterprise losing its market because of antiquated techniques, or to rejuvenate a city sliding into deterioration and decay, or to improve services for an outraged clientele in need of extraordinary efforts, or to conquer a disease, or to prevent occupation by a superior power. It is not unusual to see organizations continue on their traditional paths, despite the acknowledged hopelessness of those directions and despite the examples of success by other organizations once in similar straits, simply because they cannot acquire the means to implement remedial measures.

For some organizations, nature imposes the chief limitations on resources. People who, through a series of historical accidents, find themselves on land so poor in water and minerals that all their energies are absorbed in the daily struggle to sustain biological life dare not spare hands for longer-range projects. In order to live, they are compelled to go on as they did in the past, although they could improve their lot if they could find some slack in the system.

Far more frequently, organizations are limited less by nature than by the social environment. For example, larger competitors may undercut prices in the sales area of a smaller firm, making up the losses by higher prices in less competitive territories. The managers of the smaller firm may appreciate fully the nature of their problem and yet, lacking other markets in which to offset losses, may be compelled to continue price policies that cost them customers. Or, to take another illustration, powerful states may overrun weaker neighbors, who may be helpless in the face of overwhelming strength in spite of knowing what they would like to do. Central business districts watch their clienteles desert them for the greater convenience of suburban shopping centers, yet find themselves unable to raise the funds needed to provide the parking facilities and rapid transit required to counter this trend. Competition, in short, can render inadequate resources that were once thoroughly sufficient for the level of operations of an organization, and by the time the leaders and members appreciate their situation fully, the slack resources they might have used to alter it may be devalued by competitive factors, thus condemning the organization to persist in its old routines even though these are clearly disadvantageous and could conceivably be fatal.

Resources may also be rendered inadequate by expansion of commitments beyond the capacity of a system to fulfill them. Electric utility companies, for instance, were for years distressed by the idleness of many of their generating facilities during the summer months, when short nights greatly reduced the consumption of electrical power. The spread of air conditioning after World War II solved their problem; summer became the season of peak consumption. Added to promotion of electricity for cooking and home heating, the demand for power rose so rapidly that it outstripped the construction of new generating plants, turning a power glut into a power famine. What needs to be done is self-evident, but the sudden deficit is so massive that the lead time needed to build sufficient new facilities (especially since anti-pollution interests have mobilized) practically ensures continuation of severe problems for an uncomfortably long period. Similar difficulties have occurred in the telephone system of New York City, in quality control in automobile manufacturing, and in the management of air traffic. What critics take to be cold indifference and insistence on "business as usual" is partly the inability of organizations to act all at once on the scale required after reaching beyond capacity for huge markets.

Governments—federal, state, and local alike—are particularly plagued by the pains of stretching their efforts beyond their capacity. Governments get pushed into this distressing position easily for at least two reasons. First, the beneficiaries of public services and the people who bear most of the cost of the services frequently are not the same, so that the restraints on demands for such services are weakened. Second, the political system is not well designed for the systematic ranking of priorities; it tends instead to yield at least a little bit to everyone (though, obviously, all do not fare equally well under these arrangements). A word about each of these characteristics is in order.

The fact that governments raise money by taxation rather than by putting their services on the market for users alone to pay for if they want the services seems to suggest to some people that there is no limit to what governments can do; after all, no one can refuse to pay taxes with impunity. And since those who receive services and those who pay for them are not identical, though the two groups overlap, the recipients' sense of governmental omnipotence is reinforced. It should be noted that this general rule applies to all income levels. Welfare clients do not pay directly for the programs that serve them. It is equally true that tax benefits and advantages to wealthy companies, universities, churches, and proprietary hospitals (to name a few) permit their leaders, workers, and clients to pass along to others in the society many costs which the beneficiaries would otherwise have to bear. Everyone gets some benefits he does not pay for and pays for some benefits he does not get. The linkage between the cutting and the bleeding being so intricate and difficult to trace, few claimants on governments are deterred from asserting their claims by the costs involved.

In the marketplace, price eliminates from the pool of service- or product-demanders those who lack the money to pay for what they want. Thus—sometimes in ruthless and inequitable fashion—demand and supply are kept roughly in balance. In politics, on the other hand, elected officials rarely score points for saying "no." Their calculus is not very complex, whether or not it is right; it runs something like this: Groups denied a request that is important to them may be alienated no matter how statesmanlike an official has been in other connections or how many previous favors he has done for them. Opponents routinely search out such disaffected groups so as to aggravate their discontent by publicizing the incumbent's record and promising to do better. Alienate enough groups and you risk losing your office, especially in evenly balanced constituencies. So try to do something for everyone—at least enough to reduce your vulnerability to the opposition's charges of indifference.

All politicians understand this calculus and all, to some extent, try to accommodate each other in meeting the demands of their constituencies. Logrolling is in the interest of them all. As a result, governments end up trying to perform an exceedingly wide range of functions—spreading themselves thin over hosts of activities. In one sense, this practice is evidence that they are, however imperfectly, responsive to their electorates. But it also means that their reach often exceeds their grasp.

For they are far from omnipotent. Every dollar they take for a public service might otherwise have gone to some other private or charitable purpose; they are, in other words, engaged in a competition for finite resources. It is even possible for them, by pressing too hard for taxes, to depress some of the economic sources of their tax revenues. The scope of their activities is thus confined by their competitors and by the laws of economics, if not by other factors. They cannot do everything, even if they seem inclined to try.

Given the ceiling on their resources and the sleaziness of the filter that is supposed to screen demands, governments commonly find themselves embarked on more programs than they can adequately finance and without acceptable ways of cutting some off entirely in order to concentrate on the others. There are important exceptions to this generalization; some agencies have occasionally had money thrust upon them at a greater rate than they requested, and some have consistently received as much as they asked for. By and large, however, and particularly in domestic programs, government agencies are ordinarily compelled to make do with far less than they think they need to do a proper job.

Their clienteles, concerned more with the consequences of inadequate service than with the causes, blame the shortcomings on the alleged incompetence of the "bureaucrats." Often, however, the "bureaucrats" are fully aware of the deficiencies of their agencies but are simply powerless to do anything about them. And it sometimes happens that they grow so inured to their predicament that, if funds suddenly do become available, they have difficulty rising to the occasion, like a starving man led to a feast. Cases of this kind lend support to the impression that bureaucrats cannot change their ways.

In all these ways, resource limitations commonly bind

organizations fixedly to their established repertories of behavior. Even when the leaders and members of the organizations, as well as the critics, recognize the wisdom and the justice, if not the necessity, of change, they often find themselves powerless to bring it about.

Sunk costs. Resource limitations obviously are not confined to organizations lacking assets. From what has been said, it is clear that rich organizations may sometimes find themselves as hard put to effect changes as poor ones because they have spread their riches so thin. It may be added that rich organizations not uncommonly find themselves even more immobilized than poor ones because the former have invested so much in the status quo. They may be locked into the present by their assets, for their assets also represent sunk costs.

Any investment is a sunk cost if it is not immediately convertible into some other form. Capital investment is an illustration. But so is the acquisition of knowledge or skills or even specialized experience; these all use time, energy, and money that might have been used in other ways. Such expenditures are not quickly recoverable. They are commitments to particular things and modes of behavior.

This is not to say, of course, that all sunk costs inhibit adjustment to changing conditions. Sunk costs do not faze individuals or organizations whose resources are very great compared to the investment in question. Most people with fountain pens did not hesitate to switch to ballpoints when the latter became available, even though their old pens still had years of life in them. Nor do companies enjoying annual sales in the hundreds of millions of dollars flinch from replacing automobiles for their sales force while the existing fleets are still serviceable; relative to the volume of business, this cost may be regarded as a minor item.

Moreover, sunk costs commonly *constitute* adjustments to changing conditions. Buying the most recent technology or information is, after all, a commitment. At the time it is bought, however, and for a time afterward, such a commitment may represent a strategic innovation.

Nevertheless, in a dynamic world, obsolescence eventually afflicts most apparatus, knowledge, and skills. It seldom reduces the return on these investments to zero all at once; usually the return declines gradually. So some investments continue to earn some return for the investors and are therefore retained even though the money, time, or energy would be employed differently if the investors were starting from scratch. Although alternative commitments could bring even better returns, the cost of changing over, when the investments are expensive relative to income, prohibit such adjustments. The investors therefore struggle along as best they can with what they have, incapable of doing what they know ought to be done. What is more, in order to protect their investments, they may even try to bar others from introducing new methods, as canal companies resisted aid to railroads and railroads later resisted the competition of pipelines. Both groups had too much capital tied up in their equipment and operations to abandon it, yet they were not in a position to make themselves competitive.

One of the most graphic illustrations of the effects of sunk costs may be found in the central business districts of virtually all our older cities. Most of them were planned in the era before railroads, let alone motor vehicles. Today, they can hardly begin to accommodate motor traffic and therefore have an increasingly difficult time meeting the competition of developments on the periphery of their metropolitan areas. Massive efforts, inspired and sustained by large infusions of federal funds, have thus far failed to reverse the centrifugal tendencies of population and commerce and industry. If the centers and transport nets could be wholly rebuilt, they would doubtless be quite different from what they are. And perhaps the day will come when they will be rebuilt. Meanwhile, however, too much of our society's wealth is tied up in the old urban centers to let them go under, yet the monumental costs of wholesale reconstruction defy even the United States. People know that change is needed, but even if they could all agree on what to do, it is doubtful whether the things that need to be done could be done fast enough to save the central districts. Thanks to sunk costs, we are, in a manner of speaking, trapped by our wealth. Resource limitations on ability to change are not confined to poor organizations.

Accumulations of official constraints on behavior. Still another reason why organizations may find it difficult to change their structure or action is that they become enmeshed in bodies of public law and regulation and adjudication and in their own rules and decisions. Time adds to this vast corpus; seldom does the size contract. Not even after political revolutions are all the accumulated guidelines and prescriptions of the previous regimes discarded; it takes years to devise substitutes, and in the interim the system cannot function with nothing. Consequently, even when changes in policy are promulgated, organization members discover that they are obliged to continue many of their old practices. Really to change what people do in large organizations thus turns out to require much more than a single, simple, direct order; the full extent and ramifications of the necessary changes become evident only as each attempted innovation runs afoul of long-established prescriptions and conventions. And since the correction of such situations is ordinarily accomplished by the issuance of further rulings, it generally adds still more to the accretion of relevant papers rigidifying structure and practice.

If these accretions of constraints hinder organizational change, why are they permitted to build up? One reason is the desire to reduce the injustice and resentment caused by inconsistent applications of general rules. In complicated or morally ambiguous situations, reasonable men might reasonably go in different directions. But if obviously similar issues are continually resolved in different ways, people begin to lose confidence in the fairness of the whole system. Straining for uniformity has its own drawbacks, of course; we all demand an exercise of discretion when general rules run against us, and as many offenses may be committed in the name of consistency as in the name of independent judgment. Our society, however, is universalistic rather than particularistic in its standards of justice,[7] and indignation often runs high when the representatives of organizations act as if it were otherwise. (Indeed, these representatives themselves typically do not invite conferrals of discretion, partly because they have internalized the general preference for universal norms, but also because they do not want to be targets of intense pressures for special, discretionary benefits.) Hence, detailed specifications are laid down about how every officer and employee should act in given circumstances. That is why statutes, regulations, judicial decisions, operating manuals, and other elaborations of required forms of behavior keep growing apace. The more experience an organization acquires, the more numerous it discovers the complexities and the ambiguities of its work to be, and the more its leaders feel obliged to clarify policies and refine procedures.

In addition, distrust of organizational officers and employees is responsible for a great proportion of accumulated official constraints on their behavior. Fearing that they will use organizational moneys or properties for their private purposes, we set up elaborate accounting and auditing methods to discourage and prevent them from doing so—and then adopt expensive bonding and insurance programs because we know that some will do so in spite of the safeguards. We fear they will use their appointing powers to add friends and relatives to the payrolls regardless of qualifications, so we circumscribe their appointing authority. We suspect they will enter into collusion with contractors and suppliers, letting commissions and kickbacks rather than the welfare of the organization determine who gets the organization's business, so we specify the minutiae of contracting and purchasing procedures. We believe they may be insufficiently sensitive to demands for minority employment and training, or to community planning, or to employee safety, so we demand regulations and even statutes prescribing how these values are to be protected. We are afraid that the zeal of public servants to accomplish their objectives—to drive a pesticide out of use, say, or a pollutant out of the air or water, or a suspected criminal off the streets—will override their solicitude for citizens' rights and fair play, so we spell out the steps they must take to avoid the abuse of authority. We anticipate that the records of organizations will be manipulated, so we draw up ever more minutely detailed rules for record keeping. We know that managers once refused to bargain collectively with other employees, in both the private and the public sectors, so we prescribe for this area—and then are faced with demands for intervening in intraunion and interunion relations. We have built up licensing procedures, programs for sustaining competition, and requirements for protecting consumers and the physical environment, all based on the premise that without them organization leaders will neglect or subvert these goals. If we trusted the leaders to do what we think proper, we would never take such pains to tell them, down to the last comma, what to do and how to do it; a few general instructions would suffice. But bitter experience informs us that we cannot have confidence in everyone, and a pullulation of laws and regulations and manuals is the result.

Merely to announce or publish requirements is not enough; they have to be policed. So specialized personnel, and perhaps specialized organizational units, are assigned to make sure that the rules are obeyed. They perform their mission by issuing more guidelines and policy statements and requirements, by offering advice and opinions in advance of action to colleagues who request them, and by exposing or even disallowing actions that were taken in their sphere of responsibility and seem to them improper. Budget officers, auditors, accountants, personnel administrators, purchasing officers, public relations specialists, legal counsel, and hosts of other specialists multiply the number of specifications to be satisfied, precedents to be consulted, hurdles to be cleared, advisers to be accommodated, and reviews to be anticipated. The official constraints on behavior pile up, layer on layer.

A parallel, but different, wellspring of constraints is the desire to apply the latest knowledge to the work of organizations. In our era of the "knowledge explosion," each field of information has become so broad that only specialists can keep up with the literature, not to mention the findings and the applications of the findings. All large organizations, therefore, are obliged to employ more and more specialists and to rely on specialized advice. Each organizational unit tends to become a separate collection of specialists and must consult the others to avoid clashes and contradictions and to tap their areas of expertise. Each unit thus emerges as custodian of a part of the organization's operations, issuing directives on those functions within its province. In quest of the best and most up-to-date technical performance, organizations in this way generate still more sets of specifications governing the actions of their members.

All these cross-cutting jurisdictions and interests aggravate the difficulties of changing organizational structure or procedures or policies—not merely because they conduce to conflict, tunnel vision, and the other obstacles to change reviewed earlier, but also because so much behavior of so many different kinds has to be altered in order to change direction even slightly. One might therefore infer that the leaders of organizations, who presumably wish to steer their organizations in the directions they select, would be in the forefront of those endeavoring to reduce the multiplicity and sources of such constraints. Quite the contrary! The system is advantageous for them, too; so they are apparently as inclined to sustain it as to reform it.

The reason is this: with all these diverse elements watching over each other and restraining each other's behavior, leaders preoccupied with one organizational policy or problem can feel secure that others will not get out of hand while their attention is drawn elsewhere. In order to free themselves to concentrate on selected priorities, it is useful for them to arrange for their subordinates automatically to restrain each other. This gives the leaders a chance to pick their own preferred times, places, and issues for intervening in internal operations, and thus to nudge the whole organization toward the objectives they would like it to accomplish. Many factors beyond their control have brought about the fragmentation that produces this automatic limiting mechanism, but the reassurance it provides leaders and the opportunity it affords them to dominate their agendas instead of being dominated by them, induce even the most activist and impatient executives to perpetuate and strengthen the existing system instead of dismantling it. The accretion of official constraints on behavior therefore continues unabated in virtually all organizations, complicating the task of everyone working for change.

Unofficial and unplanned constraints on behavior. Advocates of change in organizations face even more disheartening obstacles in the form of informal and customary constraints on the behavior of members. The official constraints at least loom up as identifiable targets; fire can be concentrated on them and progress measured. But when constraints are imposed by informal groupings within an organization, or are matters of customary practice rather than explicit pronouncement, they are harder to detect and more difficult to alter—but just as binding.

The workings of informal organization in and around the formal framework of official structures need no re-

hearsal here. Restriction of output, resistance to innovation, and sabotage of opposed programs by subordinates
have all been documented in treatises and case studies.[8]
We may also take note of the gradual erosion of executive
authority to expel members from organizations by dis-
charge or other means, no matter what the official rules
say; the costs of exercising the authority are sometimes so
high that it is often more economical for a leader to retain an unwanted individual than to contend with those
who would object to his separation. Innovators bent on
introducing new methods or structures or goals, even
when the innovators occupy high positions in their organizations, have broken many a lance on these unyielding
battlements.

A single anecdote illuminates the process better than
any general statement. In New York City before air
conditioning became commonplace, municipal agencies
closed their doors an hour early on extremely hot, humid
days. Over a period of time, many of them came to shorten
the work day by an hour routinely during the summer
months. The policy was purely a humane gesture made
unilaterally by high administrative officers on their own
initiative—indeed, in violation of official provisions of
law and labor contracts.

Years later, when air-conditioning had become almost
universal in municipal offices, an incoming administration, seeking ways to increase output without increasing
expenditures, discovered this widespread informal, un-
sanctioned, and possibly illegal practice. Orders were
issued at the highest levels that henceforth the official
hours of work would be observed all year round. The result was outrage in the ranks of the municipal workers
and especially among the leaders of the more militant

civil service unions. The administration was faced by threats of job action and possible strikes. Custom had hardened into a format as rigid as law. The administration had to back away.

Interorganizational agreements. Like international treaties, agreements between organizations usually impose limitations or obligations on the members. Not all constraints, in other words, originate inside an organizations' boundaries, and change may be thwarted as effectively by interorganizational understandings as by internal obstacles.

Labor contracts are the most pertinent examples, because so many aspects of organizational life that once were considered exclusively the prerogative of management or (in the case of public employers) of sovereignty, have now become subjects of negotiation. Another incident from personnel administration in the government of New York City illustrates the point vividly.

When the Lindsay administration assumed office, it decided to put a freeze on the hiring of new staff throughout the municipal government. It did not propose to dismiss people, or to demote them, or to reduce their pay; it proposed only to let the normal processes of attrition diminish the size of the city's work force. The measure looked simple and unexceptionable. Within hours of the announcement, however, a number of public service unions were protesting vehemently. Their contracts, they pointed out, covered items like individual workloads and other conditions of work. If the size of staff contemplated by those contracts (though not spelled out in them) were not maintained but were instead permitted to dwindle, the remaining employees would have to carry heavier burdens because the agencies' responsibilities would not be correspondingly reduced. Accusations of contract vio-

lation and bad faith filled the air—and the newspapers—
and intimations of job actions and strikes flew thick and
fast. The policy was quietly laid to rest. Thus do seemingly uncomplicated actions sometimes run afoul of constraints rooted in interorganizational agreements.

Labor-management accords are not the only kinds of
contracts to which these observations apply. Exponents
of change in an organization's structure may also find
their plans upset or delayed by arrangements with competitors, commitments to suppliers and customers, pledges
to public authorities in return for licenses and permits,
promises to subcontractors and prime contractors, and so
on. To be sure, agreements can be violated or ignored,
but at the peril of the violator. Lawsuits are expensive
and drawn out, and entail the risk of losing. Credit rating
declines can be disastrous. Customers once lost seldom
return. Outraged victims may possess means of retaliation.
If morality does not impel innovators to honor old obligations, strategic considerations probably will.

What organization is without such agreements and understandings, both tacit and express? What organization
escapes the constraining effects of standing interorganizational commitments that discourage or obstruct organizational change?

SUMMARY: THE IMPROBABILITY OF CHANGE

A host of forces thus tend to keep organizations doing
the things they have been doing in the recent past, and
doing them in just the way they have been doing them.
The generally recognized collective benefits of stability
and the opposition to change based on calculations of prevailing advantage, protection of quality, and the costs of
modification furnish a thought-out foundation for resist-
ing all efforts to reshape organizations or alter their be-

havior. Furthermore, many factors weaken the ability of organizations to change by blinding members and leaders to the need for alternatives to traditional practices, by ingraining in them behavior patterns so firm that they are almost fixed, and by throwing up discouraging roadblocks (such as limitations of resources, the consequences of sunk costs, accumulations of official and unofficial constraints on behavior, and interorganizational commitments) that bind them to current arrangements. So formidable is the collection of forces holding organizations in their familiar paths that it is surprising that any changes ever manage to run the gauntlet successfully. Innovations and departures from the traditional seem unlikely to prevail over the odds against them.

This is one of the reasons why many organizations die even though, presumably, they might alter themselves as conditions demand. The presumption is more optimistic than the facts. Organizations are obviously not quite so saddled with unalterable traits as biological organisms. but they are not nearly so fluid as the presumption implies. Like other living systems, they are imprisoned in the present and often cannot change, even when the future threatens them unless they do.

Curiously, these built-in tendencies toward unvarying adherence to current design and method raise questions diametrically opposite to the one raised at the start of this chapter: If one cause of organizational demise is a battery of forces inhibiting flexible responses to dynamic environments, how does it happen that so many organizations survive as long as they do? If failure to change can be fatal, why don't more organizations succumb, and succumb sooner, to all these lethal factors?

CHAPTER 2

BUT ORGANIZATIONS DO CHANGE

CHANGE DOES OCCUR IN ORGANIZATIONS in spite of the barriers impeding it. For one thing, some forces automatically conduce to change, so that any organization managing to survive for more than a very brief period inevitably adjusts to new conditions whether its members and leaders want to or not, and, in fact, whether they know it or not. For another, the inhibitors of change, powerful as they are, can be neutralized, and often are, by strategies devised for this very purpose.

INVOLUNTARY CHANGE

Theoretically, as I have said, an organization could sustain itself forever once it gets started; it has no fixed life span. Just as a biological organism remains the same organism though every cell in its body be replaced in the course of its lifetime, so an organization can remain the same organization even though every member in it be replaced in the course of time (see Appendix). But the parallel ends here. The replacement cells in organisms are usually indistinguishable from their predecessors; the

41

replacement personnel in organizations are all a little bit different from their predecessors (and from each other), particularly if they are of different generations. Inevitably, therefore, they produce changes in their organizations. The process may be very gradual and consequently almost imperceptible to all but the most careful observer. Nevertheless, it goes on relentlessly.

Personnel turnover is characteristic of large organizations that endure for longer than very short intervals. For myriad reasons, people leave or are expelled, and organizations that persist for several human generations obviously will turn over their total membership through the years. (Indeed, the organizational potential for survival beyond the lifetimes of people is one of the major reasons for forming organizations. They are instruments for the preservation of knowledge and wealth to be passed along and accumulated by later generations, and they may also serve as lasting monuments to those who found them.) New blood comes in, no matter what anyone may prefer.

Newcomers to organizations, no matter how carefully screened, bring with them values and perceptions at least a little divergent from those prevailing among members and leaders of long standing. Society harbors a great many subcultures, technologies, and specialties, and this diversity prevents homogenization of the population. Hence, new viewpoints will creep into every organization regardless of efforts to keep them out (notwithstanding a few cases that have been remarkably successful in insulating themselves). In addition, organizations often hire personnel away from their competitors when they can, in order to get people with both training and strategic information, and such recruits bring with them some of the norms of the organizations they left. Furthermore, people looking for jobs learn what the criteria of selection are, and many applicants learn to appear to conform to those standards even though they do not fully accept them. Thus, the methods of screening never exclude all potential deviants from the organizational norms.

Above all, however, the memories that guide and drive older members of organizations lose their hold on younger members. Old fears and old aspirations take on archaic qualities for new generations. The scars of a deep economic depression, for example, may make its victims cautious, insecure; the resulting lack of daring and the eager embracement of boring but safe routines may suffer rejection and even scorn from a subsequent generation reared in comparative affluence. The enjoyment of material possessions by fathers who had few of them in their own early years does not similarly inspire sons reared in, and psychologically unsatisfied by, material abundance. Rapid economic growth can be an all-absorbing goal for people who have known the miseries of a marginal, subsistence standard of living; other goals—racial justice, ecological balance, social amenities, to mention a few— become much more salient later on, as the relative increments of benefit begin to decline and the costs rise. What seems like recent experience to one group in an organization is remote history to another. As the inexorable succession of generations proceeds, therefore, the structure and behavior of organizations also change. Oldtimers may be willing to rest on their laurels, but newcomers are impatient to win theirs.

In many organizations, the gradual changing of the guard is accompanied by tensions and conflict. The participants perceive what is happening and fight openly. Often, however, the departures of newcomers from familiar patterns are so modest as to be tolerable to older members. The small departures accumulate over time, so that the organizations change without anyone being fully aware of what is happening and without anyone even consciously willing it.

In sum, organizations accommodate to their changing environments in spite of the barriers to change because they cannot always avoid adjusting and frequently do not even know they are doing so.

VOLUNTARY CHANGE

MOTIVATIONS TO PROMOTE CHANGE

Organizations also change, however, because people deliberately change them. The motives of people who want change are very much like the motives of other people who are moved to resist change; whether an individual is inspired by these motives to agitate for reform or to stand fast on the status quo is determined by his position in, and perceptions of, the system. Many people on both sides are animated by self-interest, but it is in the self-interest of those who feel deprived to try to reconstitute things and in the self-interest of those who are advantaged to hang on to what they have. In like fashion, many who put the survival of the organization above all else will construe this value as requiring the organization to stay exactly as it is; others with the same concern will be more anxious about the jeopardy in which inflexibility allegedly places the organization, and will interpret their commitment as obliging them to foster receptivity to change. People concerned chiefly with a particular organizational feature—some aspect of output or method, for example—

will oppose all changes threatening that feature, but will vigorously promote or support changes favoring it. Even advocates of the same ends may divide over means, some perceiving prevailing arrangements as serving those ends (e.g., perceiving large, centrally-directed school systems as producing better education) while others see extensive modifications (e.g., decentralization of school administration) as the only way to accomplish the agreed-on goals.

In short, every organization is under pressure from innovators and reformers as well as from defenders of things as they are, and the motivations of the former may be of much the same character and intensity as those of the latter. The forces for change, like the forces against it, are numerous and varied. But the barriers to change described in Chapter I present formidable obstructions to the proponents of change. Whether they enjoy any success at all depends on their ability to surmount the systemic obstacles, to remove the mental blinders, and to neutralize or reverse the opposition blocking their way.

OFFSETTING SYSTEMIC OBSTACLES

Importing resources. When the prime cause of inability to change is the lack of resources to effect the measures widely recognized and agreed upon, obtaining resources from other organizations that have them in abundance is the usual way out of the dilemma. It is not an easy task. People with plentiful resources seldom have great confidence in organizations with meager assets, and they worry about pouring their own substance into futile ventures that drain the benefactors without really helping the beneficiaries. They also fear that they may be supporting their own competition. In any event, they are understandably reluctant to deprive themselves in order to assist others.

Organizations nevertheless do acquire resources from other organizations. They may have to pay exorbitant prices, it is true, in interest or shares in the returns or other concessions to the suppliers or lenders. They may resort to a kind of extortion, playing on the fears and the guilt of the richer organizations. They may be able to mobilize sufficient political support to persuade governments to assist them. Resource-poor organizations have had to become adept at every mode of persuasion.

The benefactors tend to perceive their resource-transferring programs as evidence of their own altruism and bountiful generosity. The beneficiaries are apt to describe it as self-interested and exploitative, and niggardly to boot—a bid for valuable strategic advantages at cut rates, and a largely symbolic response to urgent human needs. Nevertheless, transfers of resources continue. Rich countries send and lend funds, equipment, and supplies to underdeveloped countries. They give them technical advice and train their people in modern trades and professions so as to overcome deficiencies in skills. In the United States, corresponding programs are conducted on a growing scale to benefit our own disadvantaged groups and areas.

The dream of succeeding by nothing more than the sweat of one's own brow has not altogether vanished. The vision of owing nothing to anyone, materially or morally, for the vigor of one's organization—of being one's own boss in every sense—still has a strong appeal. Nonetheless, in today's world most people and most organizations have to seek resources from outside their own reserves in order to break the bonds of resource limitations.

Concentrating resources. An even more difficult technique of coping with resource limitations is to set priorities for the application of resources to problems and to stand by those priorities. As we have seen, in the public sector, the dynamics of the system run the other way; the thrust of the incentives is toward spreading resources over as broad a front as possible, which often allows so little for each program as to prevent the mobilization required to set out boldly in any new direction. This reality wars with the need for choice.

Furthermore, experts disagree on which activities should receive prompt attention and which should be deferred if an organization is to lift itself out of the pit of resource limitations and adjust to changing conditions. When it comes to modernizing national economies, for example some specialists will argue for concentrating on heavy industry, others give first priority to agricultural modernization, and still others believe in building consumer demand and letting the market take care of the rest. Some experts defend sequential development of selected economic sectors, holding that an economy advances itself like an amoeba, sending out salients behind which the rest of the system then flows; others urge balanced growth on a wide front. There is no consensus yet.

Moreover, the interests affected by the ordering of priorities are at odds with each other. Which ones will benefit immediately, and which ones will be deprived until some distant future? How long will consumers wait before they rebel against the allocation of resources to heavy industry in disproportionate amounts? Why modernize armies when the civilian populace is in dire need, or why capitulate to short-range, private, civilian clamor for more consumer goods when the whole system is in jeopardy from external enemies? Why improve telephones when infant mortality is still high? Even if theorists should agree on the proper choices in such situations, the people who stand to gain or lose by the decisions will not.

In authoritarian systems, policy decisions of this kind are made relatively quickly, once the leaders have committed themselves to change. In democratic systems, in which power is diffused, it is much more difficult to arrive at such decisions and to stick with them. Extraordinary feats of leadership are needed, and even extraordinary leaders may require the leverage of dangers to the whole system that are so clear and imminent as to cause contesting groups to set their differences aside temporarily, or at least to reduce the intensity of their combat.

Nevertheless, for all the difficulties and problems involved, choices are made. Despite uncertainties about the proper course of action and divisive passions set loose by priority-setting, most organizations and nations manage to chart their courses when they need to. And they succeed in mobilizing even severely limited resources to adjust to the changing environment.

Avoiding sunk costs. Limitations on resources often stem from sunk costs. Investments of any kind tie up resources that might be used in other ways, reducing degrees of freedom. If they lose their utility before their anticipated lives are over, they are especially burdensome. Therefore, when change demands an influx of resources, an organization with enormous assets in the form of massive investments may find itself in as tight a bind as one with few assets. For this reason, all organizations tend to look for ways of holding down their sunk costs.

Minimizing such costs is not easy in an industrial society, for obvious reasons. Yet three tendencies, all in early stages and small in scale, suggest that the impulse to do so is there and that the means to do so will perhaps be found someday. The first of these tendencies is the use of disposable commodities in place of durables. The second is the use of modular units that can be easily moved and recombined. The third is leasing equipment instead of buying it. All three hold down sunk costs to some extent.

Disposable, short-lived items are attractive because production of commodities is increasingly on a mass, automated basis while repair and maintenance are still essentially handicraft operations. The cost of the latter over the life of a long-lived product may exceed the cost of acquiring the product. We may thus be approaching the point where it is more economical to build cheaply and replace frequently than to keep up a well-made and long-lasting but obsolescent, expensive-to-service, and costly item. To the extent that manufactured items bind organizations to the status quo, such a shift would constitute a profoundly liberating measure. Admittedly, building cheaply and for short product lives may merely guarantee continuing markets and raise profits while lowering quality, in which event buyers will be worse rather than better off. But obsolescence may be a result of new developments, not merely of age; product durability does not necessarily stave it off. Service costs are now almost prohibitive and will continue to rise. Building in durability adds to production costs and lengthens the period of commitment to current practices. Easily replaceable apparatus is a release from these encumbrances. In spite of the risks of abuse, therefore, we will probably see more of cheap and short-lived products, and in a wider va-

49

riety of hitherto unimaginable applications, as time goes on.

The possibilities of modular design are indicated by the growing practice of putting movable walls in the interiors of office and public buildings. These permit rearrangement of the interiors as needed, at a comparatively modest cost. Extending the logic of such construction, we may envision whole buildings made up of prefabricated components that can be reconfigured when conditions warrant, and eventually replaced more inexpensively than is possible with present construction techniques. For the same reasons, we may also expect the popularity of mobile homes, classrooms, libraries, exhibits, and similar institutions to rise rapidly and the use of inflatable and collapsible furniture to increase. To be sure, the savings achieved by such practices in the present day are far from revolutionary. If the pace of societal and technological change continues at its recent levels, however, it probably is not visionary to anticipate more widespread use of such products as a means of escaping the bondage of sunk costs.

Leasing equipment instead of buying it releases organizations that do not need a particular item on a full-time basis from the necessity of tying up capital in it. The lessor, on the other hand, by leasing it to many customers and thereby keeping it in operation more of the time than any single lessee could, can afford to replace it more quickly than a single lessee could. The customers thus get better equipment than they could otherwise afford, and at the same time are able to reduce sunk costs.

Sunk costs constitute only a fraction of the barriers to organizational change, and the strategies summarized here impinge on only some of the sunk costs. In themselves, therefore, these strategies are not major liberating factors. Yet they deserve notice because they do offer some clues to future patterns of organizational behavior, as organizations search for ways to surmount barriers to change.

Lifting official constraints. In the day-to-day problems of most organizations it is probably not limited resources that seem the most inhibiting but constraints imposed by accumulations of laws, rules, and regulations. Disabling as resource shortages are to members and leaders who want to introduce change, I have the impression that most of them would be prepared to cope with these shortages if only they were emancipated from the web of requirements and surveillance in which they feel entrapped. No one ever has all the money he would like to have in order to do his job properly, but being denied discretion makes the money problems seem all the worse. Indeed, to have adequate resources but circumscribed discretion might be even more frustrating. That is why the universal plea of those who seek change is for a lifting of official constraints on their actions.

Their battle cry is, "authority commensurate with responsibility." As I understand it, the meaning is, "Turn my friends and me loose!" Or more accurately, perhaps, "Give us more independent power!" To interpret their request solely in terms of a hunger for power or a desire to escape supervision in order to improve their chances for personal gain would be unduly cynical, notwithstanding occasional corroborating instances of such motivations. Generally, a sincere eagerness to get on with the job also plays a role. At least, it is an equally plausible explanation.

For customers and clients are not the only people infuriated by the delays, the facelessness, the evasions, the timidity, and the arrogance of bureaucracies. The members of organizations who find themselves enmeshed in intricate procedures and restrictions, watched and reviewed and inspected and investigated and called to account every step of the way, are even more outraged by their inability to act with expedition and justice and common sense according to their own lights, and to adjust policies as individual situations seem to them to warrant. For them, power means more than self-aggrandizement; it means deliverance from their bureaucratic bondage, a chance to display their prowess, the possibility of changing things they believe need changing.

To put it another way, spokesmen for change ask to be trusted—trusted to attain a satisfactory balance among all the values the network of official constraints is intended to ensure, trusted not to embarrass their superiors and colleagues by actions that reflect detrimentally on them and on the organization, trusted to take advantage of the specialized knowledge and skills in the organization that can improve their performance. Procedures premised on the view that subordinates will do wrong in all these ways unless kept in check do indeed reduce the chance of error or misfeasance, but they also increase the inequities, mistakes, and sometimes disasters resulting from inaction. Errors of omission made by individuals who are immobilized by prohibitions and directives may be worse than any errors of commission they might make on occasion. Freedom to act, to exercise discretion, and therefore to alter policies, programs, and procedures implies leadership confidence in the liberated agents.

At a high level of abstraction, almost every informed commentator will sympathize with this position. In practice, however, the specific decisions about who is to be liberated are less consensual. Top management thinks the battle mottoes mean that the upper levels will be unleashed, but field personnel and interest groups with influence at local levels visualize sweeping decentralization. Every administrative echelon wants authority delegated to itself but is reluctant to delegate authority to the levels lower down. Territorial officers construe decentralization as ordaining power for them, but functional specialists read it as a Magna Charta for their offices.

Determining which participants in the life of an organization are to be released from official constraints in order to encourage organizational change depends on what changes—what policies and procedures and goals—one wants to advance. When an advocate of change knows what he wants to achieve, he will promptly agitate against the constraints that stand in the way and for broader discretion to those who will help him to realize his ends. Much of the energy allocated to lifting official constraints is therefore concentrated on particular provisions of the existing corpus of law and regulation. As a general principle, however, all contestants subscribe to the idea of broader discretion, and conceivably to the concept that more discretion for everyone, not just themselves, might be salutary. The strictures of accumulated weight lie heavy on all.

Efforts to throw off this weight are partly responsible for the rapid increase in the number of public corporations, or mixed public-private corporations, in American government in recent years. Both new and old public functions have been turned over to them (as exemplified by both Comsat and the venerable old Post Office), including housing, transportation, urban renewal, and hos-

pitals. Neighborhood development corporations are bur-
geoning. In the more distant future, education, health,
and natural-resource management may go the same route.
Corporations have appeared and flourished at the local,
state, federal, and even international levels. Including
the profusion of "special districts," many of which are
public corporations, the number of these agencies is impressive and growing fast.

The advantages of the public corporation over the
traditional bureau reside in the former's exemption
from the restraints that envelop the latter. Hemmed in
by jurisdictional limitations, by elaborate procedural requirements with regard to finances, personnel, purchasing, and other housekeeping chores, and by the hazards
and detailed controls of the appropriations process, bureaus often cannot accomplish the missions given them.
The corporate form generally excepts a government
agency from many of these obligations, while leaving it
with the powers and the public-interest perspective that
motivate governmental assumption of the function. For
this reason, it is becoming an increasingly popular instrument; the layers of safeguards and commands that contain the discretion of bureaus have unfitted them for the
tasks that now confront them, forcing the designers of
governments to employ a relatively new device to get out
from under.

Reorganizing. Yet another way of upsetting systemic
obstacles to change is reorganizing. This is commonly de-
fended in terms of rationalizing disorderly administrative arrangements, improving efficiency, "streamlining,"
coordinating, and promoting similarly favored engineer-
ing concepts and images of symmetry. More realistically,
Simon, Smithburg, and Thompson have explained the

practice in terms of redistributing influence and emphasizing different values.[1] As a weapon in the arsenal of change-seekers, it works by disrupting established lines of access and other regularities that keep people doing the old things in the old ways. In the interval of uncertainty about relationships and practices that follows any reorganization, those who want to break away from old norms may be able to introduce new behavior patterns that could never take root without a prior disturbance of the habitual arrangements. Reorganization is frequently nothing more than a "shake-up" intended to loosen the system a little.

In particular, reorganizations unsettle those unofficial and unplanned constraints on behavior that constitute the "informal organization" and cannot be readily reached by other means. These inertial forces are hard to identify and are hard to counteract even when they are identified. Occasionally, when the advocates of change discern that an informal group or liaison stands in their way, they may try to neutralize it by coopting its most active members into their own camp. By and large, though, the informal system is shadowy and elusive, and reorganization is an appealing way of dealing with it because a reorganization can upset the informal system without explicitly identifying it.

Reorganization is not without its risks to the changes sought by those who employ it. While the temporary disarray and confusion may create opportunities to advance favored plans as against ongoing practices, they also afford opportunities to competing innovators. And even in the absence of competition, reorganizations often produce wholly unanticipated effects; that is why the results of so many reorganizations are so at variance with the aims of their sponsors. Creating a better *climate* for change does not always produce only the change one wants.

Nevertheless, reorganizing is a popular strategy with proponents of organizational change who run up against the deep-rooted, customary modes of behavior. Apparently, they prefer the possibility of undesirable change to the certain objectionable consequences of staying put.

Taking Off Mental Blinders

The assaults on the systemic obstacles to change are directed at factors "external" to the individuals who make up organizations. In contrast, strategies for taking off mental blinders seek to overcome sources of resistance that are primarily "inside" each individual.

Recruiting unorthodoxy. Some organizations, uneasy about the dangers of inadaptiveness, try to assure themselves of innovative pressures by deliberately scouting for recruits with unorthodox viewpoints and ways of thinking. For all the reasons noted in the previous chapter, heterodoxy is not and cannot be characteristic of the great majority of new members and leaders; most of them must be fitted into the ongoing system. Even so, executives and personnel managers concerned for the future as well as with the present typically search for minds untrammeled by the conventions of their organizations. They may isolate these people in planning units or confine them to advisory capacities rather than put them in positions of formal authority, but they do not deprive themselves of the options to which the unconventional people may alert them.

Recruiting unorthodoxy does not consist in hiring individuals whose behavior or dress is bizarre, though it does imply some tolerance for the exotic. Creative minds seldom signal themselves in such fashion. Neither is there any test or battery of tests that reliably identifies the creative person; the elements of creativity elude description and measurement. Opinions of referees who know a candidate well, understand what is wanted of him, and have some objectivity are usually a better guide. Still better is a record of his past performance. At best, however, finding and engaging imaginative, original thinkers is a difficult, uncertain undertaking.

A simpler way to add members and leaders not locked into an organization's entrenched patterns is to recruit at least some members from trades and professions other than the ones predominant in the organization. Not that the other trades and professions are any freer of mental blinders; far from it. But they have different blinders, which produce some different perceptions, assumptions, and values. Occupational variations in an organization may thus provoke diverse ideas and constructive tensions. Similarly, representation of various geographical areas, social classes, ethnic groups, and educational backgrounds benefits an organization above and beyond the satisfaction of democratic ideological objectives; it engenders an atmosphere in which multiple viewpoints and interests can counterbalance the impulses toward a rigid and deadening consensus.

Recruiting unorthodoxy also implies some degree of "lateral entry" into the upper ranks of the organization (as opposed to promotion from within almost exclusively). If the upper ranks are filled entirely by members who have served in the lower ranks, they will be populated by individuals who have internalized the organization's norms and thus lost some of their freshness of viewpoint and unconventionality. "New blood" must be brought in at all levels if a strategy of cultivating heterodoxy is to be effective.

And, finally, it implies the wisdom of assembling at least several unorthodox people in each distinctive grouping or specialty. The lone deviant, with no one to reinforce him, will feel too powerless to impress his views on the system and too insecure to cleave to those views. Experimental evidence indicates that social pressures induce outward conformity with group consensus, even when the consensus is clearly wrong, and suggests that the conformity may even be inward as well as outward; the isolate is apparently likely to become more conventional than anyone else.[2] Thus, if representatives of varied backgrounds are brought into organizations in order to encourage nonconforming contributions to decision-making processes, the purpose will be defeated unless the number of nonconformists attains some "critical mass." To be sure, they may be most conventional in their own small circles, but in the larger context they are not, and they will not retain their unconventionality long if they must hold out alone against the larger context.

Training and retraining. Recruiting heterodoxy is not really a way of taking the mental blinders off an organization's leaders and members in general; rather, it is a way of adding to the organization's roster some people on whom the systemic blinders were never imposed. However, no organization can depend exclusively on recruitment to keep the doors open to the winds of change. Therefore many organizations, and especially large ones, maintain training programs that encourage and assist originality on the part of conventional members who show some promise in that direction. If this wording sounds a bit skeptical, it is because the exigencies of day-to-day operations tax the capacity of organizations to train people to perform even the normal routines; as I observed in Chapter I, most training is intended to fit people into ongoing systems. It would therefore be surprising if time, money, and inclination to make nonconformists of members who already meet some systemic needs were provided abundantly and enthusiastically in most organizations. Yet there is no doubt that it has become established practice in some organizations to try to broaden horizons, at least at the leadership levels. In conferences, seminars, and discussion groups, formally constituted or gathering informally, exchanges of views have become ways of challenging received wisdom and stimulating imagination.

Ultimately, however, when insiders educate each other they soon lapse into confirming traditional lore. Organizations that want to broaden horizons therefore rely much more heavily on outside stimuli. They deliberately expose their up and coming leaders to extraorganizational ideas.

Exposure to extraorganizational ideas. The usual way of exposing leaders in organizations to extrinsic intellectual influences is to bring them into contact with academics working in the same or related areas. The university, after all, is supposed to be not only the custodian of past knowledge but also the generator of new knowledge. Professors are accustomed to addressing groups brought together for pedagogic purposes. Under the pressures and incentives of their occupational standards, they write the treatises that embody and summarize the most recent findings in their fields and therefore presumably are qualified to instruct and inspire groups too preoccupied with day-to-day operations to keep abreast of recent developments in appropriate disciplines. The professors' schedules are flexible, so they tend to be more available for appearances than most people who ply other trades. For these reasons, organizations intent on avoiding narrow parochialism, stodginess, and obsolescent information in their leadership groups have adopted all sorts of measures to expose them to the wisdom of academics.

The old-fashioned method is to recognize advanced training with higher job classifications and salaries; the organization supplies only the incentive, leaving the initiative and the expense to the employee. More recently, organizations have assumed more and more of the burdens of arranging, or at least paying for, the exposure. They set up seminars, bringing in academics to lecture to, and lead discussions among, the organizations' members. Or they send their personnel to training institutes, where the trainees, housed together for weeks at a time, are offered concentrated diets of seminars and lectures; the advantage of such institutes is that they can operate on a larger scale because they draw their students from many different organizations, so that the net cost to each participating organization is lower, and the quality of the syllabus and the faculty is presumably higher, than those which any individual organization could achieve if it ran its own program. Some organizations have even adopted the principle of the "sabbatical"—or extended period of leave with pay—so that selected members can attend a university or sojourn with a research institution, refreshing mind and spirit away from the deadening routines and pressures of the job.

These practices are increasingly expensive, but they seem to be spreading despite rising costs. Do they really work? Do they actually lift the blinders from personnel who would otherwise lose their edge? Appraising the results of any form of higher education is always a troublesome task. We know that these expensive activities, which deprive organizations of some of their key people for extended periods of time, win the acquiescence, if not the enthusiastic approval, of hardheaded executives, legislators, and businessmen. Perhaps that is the best answer we can give. At any rate, in order to keep themselves adaptive and au courant, organizations do employ these means, effective or not. For these purposes, evidently, uncertain instruments are judged better than none.

They are not the only instruments, however. Even organizations of only modest size maintain working libraries, circulate periodicals, call attention to relevant new publications. They commission studies by consultants. They encourage and fund attendance by their members at meetings of professional societies. They maintain their own research units. Wherever there is a stream of ideas that impinges on their activities, they try to dip into it. And thus they try to fight against the closing of minds that helps render organizations incapable of change.

REDUCING INCENTIVES TO OPPOSE CHANGE

Strategies aimed at increasing the ability of people in an organization to change its structure or behavior deal with factors that would inhibit change even if everyone in the organization wanted to change. Many of them, of course, do not want change—not necessarily because they are afflicted with mental blinders or because they cannot make headway against the systemic obstacles but because change imposes on them costs they would not otherwise have to bear. The status quo rewards them; the new situation would penalize them. Quite sensibly, under these conditions, they resist change even when it is possible.

Simon, Smithburg, and Thompson, analyzing the methods of obtaining compliance with organizational policy on the part of an organization's clientele, set out an inventory of procedures equally applicable in principle to *all* sources of calculated resistance.[3] They describe the kinds of costs that often arouse resistance and the steps by which these costs can be reduced. They suggest, for example, ways to make compliance easy, so that the costs of modifying longstanding habits are lowered; ways to identify proposed innovations with widely accepted values so as to minimize the moral costs of obedience to changes about which many people may have ethical misgivings; ways to cut self-interest costs by minimizing disturbance of prevailing practices and relations; to diminish "rationality costs" by carefully developing and communicating acceptable justifications of the innovations; and ways to reduce "subordination costs" by consultations with affected parties so that they do not feel as though they are being pushed around. Simon and his colleagues also review the techniques by which acceptance of change can be made more rewarding than opposition, such as conferring legitimacy on the new way of acting, deliberately developing informal as well as formal penalties for violations of the new norms, and broadening the range of inducements to comply with new requirements.

I shall not rehearse their analysis in detail. I will pause, however, to elaborate a little on one of their points especially relevant to what I have said about calculated opposition to change. They observe that often the victims of change can be compensated for their losses and thus induced to abandon their opposition. This is as true within an organization as it is in the organization's dealings with its clientele. Pension systems or high-paying sinecures, for example, may motivate people to make room for new blood in key positions. Union welfare funds financed out of increased profits from technological innovations may be used to maintain the incomes of workers laid off as a result of technological improvements, thereby eliminating one reason for the workers to oppose the improvements. (Since many work incentives are not financial, this strategy seldom eliminates all opposition, however. Nor does it alter the incentives of union leaders, whose power at bargaining tables, in the councils of union national and international headquarters, and in politics is associated directly with the size of their memberships. The interests of the leadership are by no means identical with the interests of the rank and file.) To reduce resistance to personnel reclassification plans, it is standard operating procedure to guarantee that no one's pay will be diminished if the plans are adopted, and sometimes, indeed, everyone is offered a pay increase to sweeten a potentially bitter pill. In some situations, needless positions may be added to a reorganization plan in order to provide titles and status for influential leaders who would otherwise oppose the plan.

Appealing to self-interest in these ways is likely to be less successful when the chief reason for opposition is concern about the future quality of the organization's service or product, or about the future security and character of the organization itself. Reassuring such opponents that neither the well-being and character of the organization nor the excellence of its output will be adversely affected by the recommended change is the only way to quiet their opposition. Writing special provisions to safe-guard those values, granting veto rights to members of the opposition, assigning operation of the revised system to people trusted by the opposition, and limiting the pe-riod in which the changes are valid (thereby requiring the proponents to obtain extensions if they want the changes to continue, and automatically giving the opposi-tion new chances to block adoption) are among the tactics by which such reassurance is provided. The Constitution of the United States, for example, probably would have failed of adoption had it not been for the addition of the Bill of Rights. Osteopaths responded to opposition to their methods on the part of medical doctors by including substantial amounts of standard medical training in their professional schools, and by agreeing to high standards of licensure. The legislation giving the President authority to reorganize the executive branch of the government would have been defeated had its statute not originally had only a two-year life and provided for a congressional veto of any reorganization plans proposed by the Presi-dent. From the point of view of proponents of change, such steps to reassure opponents weaken the reforms they urge. But people who resist changes on grounds of principle are usually the most determined of all adver-saries, and meeting their objections so as to remove or reduce their incentives to fight is therefore of exceptional strategic importance. Some observers will regard the prin-cipled resisters of specific proposed changes as stubborn, narrow-minded, self-righteous diehards; others will see them as heroic defenders of the faith; but in either case, the fate of innovations frequently hinges on the elimi-nation of their opposition's incentives to prevent adoption.

Of course, organizational loyalty can sometimes be invoked to shame opponents into silence, if not to obtain their support of change; appeal to "principle" is not a single-edged instrument. But the argument that you are demonstrating loyalty to a system by laboring to change it is subtler and more complicated than the steadfast defense of the system as it stands. Therefore, innovators usually have to make their case in other terms.

Reducing the incentives to oppose change is ordinarily a different order of strategy than offsetting systemic obstacles and removing mental blinders. The last two methods may be urged by advocates of organizational flexibility to create a more favorable atmosphere for *any* kind of change rather than particular, specified changes; employing these methods may facilitate changes which the spokesmen for flexibility might themselves oppose. Thus, for instance, procedures for amendment were included in the Constitution even though they entailed the risk that the Constitution would be changed in ways the framers never intended; ensuring the capacity to change the document in *some* way was clearly considered a lesser danger than preventing unwise change by prohibiting *all* change.

The methods of removing incentives to resist change, by contrast, are usually directed against specific targets. The sponsors of change, knowing why particular individuals line up against them, contrive to render those reasons nugatory. Only those individuals and those reasons are affected (except incidentally); the general climate is made no more hospitable to other kinds of change than it ever was. Chances are, however, the more limited strategy is the most commonly employed and perhaps the most successful one.

"THE EVER-WHIRLING WHEEL OF CHANGE"

Taken all together, the factors making for change in organizations turn out to be strong enough to overcome the powerful forces against it. Some of these factors are generated by circumstances over which human beings individually and collectively have no control; willy-nilly, circumstances bring change about. Others are the planned efforts of people, some designed to prevent generally the kind of ossification that can hurt an organization, some calculated to attain a more limited end. Plans of the first kind lessen the obstacles to changes of all kinds, plans of the second kind reduce only those obstacles to specific proposals for reform. Collectively, they make it possible for organizations to survive even in environments in flux.

This assessment of forces brings us back to the questions with which we started. If organizations can and do change, why should any of them ever die because they fail to do so? If the blinders are taken off at least partially, if systemic obstructions are surmounted, if incentives to resist are neutralized, if some adjustment takes place automatically, and if there are individuals and groups in virtually every organization who, for reasons of their own, perceive the need for change and labor to accomplish it, it is surprising that all organizations do not manage to avoid the unpleasant and even lethal consequences of rigid adherence to their old forms and ways.

Obviously, the thrust toward change and the checks on it are fairly evenly matched. It is tempting to fall back on a physical metaphor and declare that every action produces an opposite reaction that is sometimes equal (in which case nothing changes) and sometimes slightly weaker (in which case some changes occur). In fact, how-

ever, organizational realities appear to be more complicated than that. Proposed changes not only encounter the
conservative tendencies surveyed in the first chapter; they
also bring into play another group of factors. To these
I turn in the next chapter.

CHAPTER 3

WHY CHANGE IS DAMPED

AFTER AN ORGANIZATION HAS BEEN CHANGED even a little, it begins to freeze into its new pattern almost at once; it does not remain loosely structured and flexible. All the tendencies that inhibited change in its prior configuration promptly make themselves felt in the new one. Furthermore, a set of forces limiting the extent and speed of change begins to take effect. These forces can be grouped in three categories: limitations on change engendered, curiously, by pursuit of the strategies for change; limitations growing out of an organizational aversion to unpredictable events; and limitations arising from the nature of the relationship between organizations and their environments.

CONSTRICTIONS GENERATED BY STRATEGIES FOR CHANGE

RESOURCES AND RIGIDITY

Resources imported to release the straitjacket imposed by resource inadequacies bring with them constraints on the discretion of the recipients of the very kind from which strategies for lifting constraints are intended to free them. It makes no difference whether the resources are lent or given by, or extorted from, the suppliers; the suppliers almost always gain influence—power to command or veto—in consequence of their actions.

Lenders, for example, begin to worry about their loans, and to intervene in the operations of the borrowers when the policies of the borrowers seem to jeopardize the lenders' interests. As a last resort, they may seize the assets, by legal or illegal means. In order to hold off foreclosure, borrowers may submit to lenders' demands on policy matters. If they do, the borrowers may find themselves in a new prison as confining as the lack of resources that drove them into debt. Indeed, sometimes the new prison is worse than the old.

Organizations that elicit "gifts" (whether freely given or extorted) may likewise find themselves in the grip of their "benefactors." If what they receive requires expertise to operate it or maintain it or repair it, and the recipients lack the needed skills and knowledge, they find they must go back to the donors for more equipment, supplies, personnel, and training. In this way, even unwilling donors may gain the upper hand, at least in relations among nations; extortioners may render themselves dependent on their prey. More commonly, the donors know exactly what they are doing, and their apparent generosity or submission turns out to be quite costly to the "beneficiaries" or "victors." Narcotics vendors were not the first to discover the advantages of taking initial losses in order to addict their customers and to reap the benefits the supplier holds over the dependent customer.

Members of societies and organizations who seek resources to effect change, and suppliers who respond to their requests, are often surprised to find that the new resources have intensified old rigidities instead of loosening or changing fixed patterns. One reason is that the resources tend to flow into established channels, where they profit and strengthen the existing leadership; the old leaders may thus be equipped with new opportunities to reinforce their entrenched positions. Another reason is that all of us are less informed than we think we are about the consequences of bestowing resources on poverty-stricken organizations and societies, and the influx of particular kinds of well-intentioned benefits may aggravate the very problems that prevent change. For example, the importation of medical and hygienic knowledge and skills without accompanying birth-control techniques by poor countries with high birth and death rates led to sharp reductions of the death rates only, producing a population surge. The population increases offset improvements in agricultural production. The net result was a larger population at the same level of want, still oppressed by a grinding poverty blocking its efforts to modernize. Similarly, infusions of money intended to improve urban centers may have raised population densities in those areas and thus added to the problems already afflicting cities instead of alleviating them.

But even if new resources do not reinforce old rigidities, every incremental investment of resources constitutes an addition to sunk costs. This is particularly true of resources made available by setting priorities. Once an order of preferences is set, it is a hostage to the future; unless the chosen sequence is strictly adhered to, oscillation from one hierarchy of priorities to another will follow, which has the same effect as having no priorities at all and trying to do everything at once. As I observed earlier, this wavering causes many resource shortages and their attendant inflexibilities. To stick firmly to a given order of preferences, in turn, requires rejection of claims and demands in conflict with the chosen plan. Authority, force, and mental conditioning will therefore be applied to forestall vacillation. Moreover, the commitment of scarce resources to any given schedule of activities pre-empts their use for other purposes. In this way, liberating resources by choosing any particular list of priorities closes off other options and fixes an organization on what may be a new, but is certainly an equally rigid, course.

Resorting to disposable, easily replaceable, highly portable goods likewise entails restraints as well as new leeways. After all, commitment to a life style that is theoretically easy to modify bars many avenues of action and organization that would otherwise be possible; persevering in that style forecloses all alternatives. Peoples who developed systems unburdened by heavy material sunk costs, such as the American Indians and the Bedouins, indeed exhibited strong resistance to change, which is why they retained many of their distinctive attributes. If avoidance of sunk costs becomes a central consideration in the design and operation of organizations, these organizations prove to be no more exempt from the tendencies against change than do organizations with heavy sunk costs despite the obvious differences in style. Inexpensive, shortlived items can free-up systems in marginal ways, but they cannot deliver organizations from constraints on a large scale.

In the end, none of the ways of trying to escape from resource insufficiencies and sunk costs can free organizations and societies from such obstacles to change for very long. To be sure, the momentary freedom can be most important, but attaining it brings new constraints in its wake.

RIGIDITY AND THE DIFFUSION OF DISCRETION

If all the accumulated laws, regulations, rules, orders, decisions, and other formal constraints on the behavior of people in organizations were repealed, what would happen? Undoubtedly, a great many changes would occur, although for a time many people would probably go on acting much as they did before. Before long, however, it is likely that most people, individually and collectively, would soon find themselves encased in a fresh (yet familiar) body of constraints engendered by their new situation and no less binding than the old one.

For, as political theorists have argued for thousands of years, the formal constraints curbing some of the discretion of people in organizations also expands their discretion in other directions. Confining the power of some individuals and groups permits others to exercise freedoms that would otherwise be denied them. Compelling some individuals and groups to do what they would otherwise not do (admit students regardless of race, for instance) opens choices for others. So removing an accumulation of formal constraints would not necessarily result in a system more amenable to change; it would merely allow *different* sets of constraints to take effect. This is not to imply that it makes no difference to the people involved which sets of constraints are in force. But it does suggest that the very act of lifting formal constraints subjects people to other requirements just as compelling and just as inflexible in their own right.

That is why decentralization of administrative power,

whether to lower-level functional specialists or to territorial officers, seldom makes an organization more flexible than it was when it was more centralized. Decentralization facilitates variation in the organization, and this may be a force for change. At the same time, since small localized units are likely to be more homogeneous than more inclusive ones, decentralization gives freer play to constricting parochial interests and local consensus, muting the clash of interests and ideas that animates participants in larger arenas. That is to say, the local representative of a big organization, hemmed in by the rules and regulations and staff agencies of levels above him, may be freer in many ways than the local representative of more nearly unanimous local powers. Local pressures are often more stifling than central ones. Decentralization is not necessarily a passport to flexibility.

Nor does creation of new organizational forms afford a long-lasting release. For example, government corporations tend to fall quickly into fixed patterns despite their exemption from limitations imposed on regular bureaus. Three clienteles are especially important to them: the banking interests who market their bonds, the buyers of their bonds, and the users of their facilities and services who furnish the revenues that make their bonds salable. Without these kinds of support most of the corporations would never get off the ground, even with government guarantees of their loans and with government loans to get them started. Hence, the officials of the corporations are often reluctant to undertake activities, adopt policies, or make structural changes that might alienate their supporters, and it takes exceptional pressure to overcome their caution.

These officials are also once removed from the alternations of political control that introduce new values and perceptions and interests into the machinery of government. In one sense, of course, this security allows them considerable autonomy for innovation, since they can take action with less fear of removal from office and other types of retribution than is felt by many of their regular bureau counterparts. At the same time, it insulates them from some of the winds of change and enables them to hew to their established practices and their longstanding accommodations with their main interest groups. They are therefore vulnerable to a set of forces constricting their capacity to alter their behavior.

If I may digress for a moment from my main line of argument, let me add parenthetically that the fate of government corporations repeats the history of other governmental organs on which power was devolved in order to permit governments as entities to respond flexibly to new situations. When the English courts of common law became mired in their centuries of precedents, relief was provided by the courts of equity, rooted in the discretion of the king and his chancellor rather than in prior decisions of judges. As the courts of equity became fully "judicialized" over time, the legislative body furnished responses less bound by the past. When the demands of industrial society required still greater speed, flexibility, continuity, and uniformity than legislative procedures could maintain, more and more discretion was conferred on administrative bureaus; in modern states, more legislation and adjudicative decisions (although kept within boundaries defined by legislatures and courts) emanate from administrative bodies than from the legislatures and the courts. The increasing use of the public corporation in turn grew out of the weight of amassed formal constraints

upon bureaus and other traditional agencies. The rigidification of the new instrument follows a wellworn path:
the very devices to which governments resort to facilitate
adaptation to new conditions grow fixed in their own
patterns. And the additional institutions further compli-
cate systems already too complex to change readily.

Thus, as soon as measures intended to lift the load of
accumulated constraints are put into effect, they turn loose
a host of other constraints equally inhospitable to change.
The new rigidity may be more satisfying to more people,
at least for a while, but it will be every bit as rigid as the
old one.

Personnel Management and Orthodoxy

The same thing happens when organization leaders concerned about adaptability succeed in attracting personnel
unfettered by the conventions of the system. The new
types begin at once to exert pressure for more kindred
spirits in order to reform the system; the old personnel
continue in the old paths. Gradually, at least in their own
sections, the new staff assembles a corps of likeminded
people. Fired by a sense of shared mission and shared
risks, they become a tight-knit clique. By the time the
clique moves into strategic positions in the organization,
its members have evolved common principles and outlooks, a body of doctrine all their own, which eventually
are incorporated into the norms of the organization as a
whole.

Having themselves employed such strategies as foot-
dragging, evasion, and noncompliance to advance their
cause, the new leaders feel the need to protect themselves
against the use of the same techniques by those who oppose them. They insist on tight screening for consistency

with their own ideas, careful and extensive indoctrination of their aides, and promotion of only the demonstrably loyal. In no time at all, they have introduced an orthodoxy every bit as confining as the one they modified.

Meanwhile, personnel offices and agencies, whose ability to survive depends on their success in marketing the products of their recruiting, screening, and training programs, either adapt their practices to the new requirements or are replaced by others that do. In time, there is a personnel-administrative establishment that reinforces the new criteria. Its members serve the purposes of the modified organization by feeding it people who meet its current needs, whereupon they become defensive of the new criteria that they have learned to serve so well.

Hence, as soon as an organization begins to remove the mental blinders from its leadership and membership in the ways described in the preceding chapter, it lays the groundwork of an even stricter conformity.

REORGANIZATION AND CHANGE

Like the other strategies for change, reorganization stimulates its own limiting forces, but often, unlike the other strategies, does not change the system much before its progress is checked. When the smoke and dust of the battle attending most structural changes settle, many organization members discover that nothing seriously interferes with their impulse to go on doing just what they were doing previously.

In some ways, however, reorganization makes change *more* difficult than it was before. Reorganization often results in layering—the piling of administrative echelon upon administrative echelon in an unremitting quest for coordination, symmetry, logic, and comprehensible order. As soon as the incumbents in newly created or modified command positions find their footing, they build their respective staffs and commence to exert an influence on their organizations through new orders, directives, instructions, guidelines, interpretations, decisions, clearance, reviews, vetoes, etc. A new source of administrative issuances is added to all the old ones, formulating new constraints, both procedural and substantive. Another set of staff offices goes into action. The time it takes a subordinate officer to get a firm decision from his superior is extended. All recommendations for change have to run a longer, more trying, more deadly gauntlet.

Layering also stretches lines of communication. It gets harder and harder for the highest-level executives to influence their nominal subordinates many levels below, and they get such compressed and summarized and filtered information from below that they may be only dimly aware of the effects of their efforts at leadership. Yet it is to the top levels that advocates of change are usually compelled to carry their battles for innovation, because the systemic inertial forces that bind the lower and intermediate levels prevent change at these levels. That is, by attenuating the influence of leaders while adding to the bonds on subordinates, the layering of echelons in the course of reorganization can slow down innovation instead of speeding it along.

Finally, layering generally hampers the recruitment of fresh talent for positions "demoted" as a result of reorganization. An individual who could be attracted to an office with direct access to the chief executive of an organization might well hesitate to accept a position one level removed, and he might be repelled by one still more remote than that. Consolidating and "streamlining" thus makes a small number of posts highly attractive and a large number much less attractive than they were.

In these circumstances, leaders may be forced to reach into the permanent ranks of the subordinate units for unit chiefs instead of bringing in new blood. Reorganization can in this fashion increase the hold of insiders who are socialized to the organization's time-honored procedures and policies. Instead of creating an atmosphere encouraging to change, it may thereby do just the opposite. I do not contend that this happens every time, of course, but it does seem to me that these constricting forces are stimulated when reorganizations regroup constituent elements of large administrative structures and sharply limit whatever liberating effects the shake-up may have.

How Reducing Calculated Opposition to Change Constricts Change

Virtually every strategy for reducing incentives to oppose change involves compromise on the extent of the changes proposed. In order to make the departures *seem* less substantial than they are, it is often necessary to make them *actually* less sweeping than they would otherwise have been. Getting changes accepted in this way automatically limits the extent of reform; the more extreme the proposals, the more resolute the opposition and the greater the need for compromise. The technique has its own built-in dampers.

Compensating the victims of change, for example, typically entails costs that divert resources from implementation of the innovations and thus reduce the scale of reform. Similarly, moderating the scope and character of changes is often the only way to persuade opponents concerned about the quality of goods or services that the changes are acceptable. Reducing incentives to oppose change may mean reducing change itself.

Knowing this, advocates of change are impelled to ask for more than they know they can get, hoping the compromise will fall closer to their real aspirations. The opposition, being no less shrewd as game theorists, naturally takes a more intransigent position at the outset than it intends to settle for. Consequently, the settlement ends up about where it would have if both sides had been less calculating to begin with. Since neither side can be sure the other will play that way, however, each feels that it must protect its interests by taking more extreme positions than it really insists on.

No matter how an innovator tries to reduce calculated opposition to change, his strategy will always curb its own radicality.

Self-limiting Change

In a sense, then, organizational change is a self-limiting process. That is one reason why equilibrium and steady-state and homeostatic models are so intuitively persuasive. The degree of change is circumscribed not merely by the inherent tendencies always pressing to keep things as they are, but also by inhibitors which the forces of change themselves activate. They carry the seeds, as it were, of their own containment.

AROUSAL OF ORGANIZATIONAL AVERSION TO UNPREDICTABILITY[1]

Reason for the Aversion

The constrictions generated by the strategies for change are uniquely tied to those specific strategies. In addition, introducing change into an organization stimulates certain more general factors of rigidification, for change excites anxieties in the many people whose personal security and docility are rooted in the steady and predictable environment provided for them by their organizations.

Organizations buffer their members and suborganizations from the effects of sudden variations in the timing, intensity, and direction of flows and events affecting their well-being. Such shifts are more than merely distressing; they can be downright threatening. Quite apart from the other collective benefits of stability, the comforting assurance that the immediate environment will not change significantly all at once accounts in part for the willingness of people to put up with the irritants to which life in organizations subjects them. Despite the potential fallacies of reasoning from organism to organizations, the point may be illustrated by citing the environmental conditions of the cells in a body as against those of the single-celled organism fending for itself; the tolerance of either for variations in temperature, chemical environment, and the like, is not great, but the body shelters the former from variations, keeping the surroundings almost constant, while the latter has no such cushion. In a crudely analogous way, organizations shelter the people and groups who form their substance. No one takes kindly to anything that disturbs this shelter.

INDICATORS OF THE AVERSION

We can see evidences of aversion to unpredictability in the way human organizations behave with respect to uncertainties beyond their boundaries (sources of supplies, say, or the activities of competitors). At first, they merely accommodate to such uncertainties as best they can, passively reacting to whatever the environment inflicts or bestows on them; these are conditions of maximum unpredictability. Gradually, they try to detect patterns, so as to anticipate and prepare for developments affecting them; by improving their predictions, they can accommodate more actively. In time, they move on toward control, making the events outside their boundaries partially subject to stimuli from inside. Eventually, they begin to approach total control. Each shift along the continuum from accommodation to control improves predictability and reduces uncertainty, until nothing happens with respect to the controlled variable unless the leaders of the organization will it. No organization has ever established total control over anything, including its own internal processes, but once the march along the continuum has begun it tends to go on indefinitely and to gain momentum as it goes.

By way of illustration, take foodgetting by human societies. Initially, they adjusted passively to the bounty of nature, taking fruit and vegetables and game wherever and whenever they happened to find them. As they perceived regularities in the cycles and behavior of their supplies, they commenced to seek them out and harvest them systematically; more accurate predictions meant more efficient food gathering, less uncertainty, and a less precarious existence. Then came the first controls: deliberate domestication of plants and animals. Though the crops and herds were at first still governed more by nature than men in most regards, more and more factors were gradually brought under human control: moisture, breeding, feeding, disease, and other enemies of food supply. Even light. And the declining oscillations of supply were further smoothed out by improved methods of preservation. We can now watch the techniques of controlling food supply being extended to marine sources, which are still in much earlier stages of development than land sources. The battle against unpredictability goes on endlessly. Wherever any vestige remains and impinges on an organization, the organization moves to reduce it, eventually by bringing the causes under control.

Not all sources of external uncertainty are natural (i.e., nonhuman). Some uncertainties arise because of relations with other organizations. If two organizations are linked in a chain of processes that permits either to deprive the other of something it requires to continue functioning (supplies, for example, or markets), both will be uneasy. Or if they both want to control the same people or objects or activities, each will be anxious about what the other is likely to do.

They can try to accommodate to each other, but that is not likely to be a permanent solution. It is too uncomfortable. Rather, they begin to edge toward the control end of the continuum as soon as they acquire sufficient strength to justify any realistic hope of success. If not, they may join with the others in submitting to some more inclusive organization that exerts some controls over them all. Short of that, they at least try to stabilize relations among them by agreements and understandings. (Occasionally, some even move in the other direction, in quest of isolation from the sources of anxiety through attempts at self-sufficiency. I shall come back to this later on.) That is why international organizations, cartels, trusts, and similar arrangements are formed even in the face of powerful opposition. And why corporate giants and conglomerates reach out in all directions. And, finally, why organizations always seem to distrust other organizations.

Many sources of uncertainty, of course, are not external to organizational boundaries at all; they occur within. Individuals, informal groups, and suborganizations display varying degrees of autonomy at different times, on different matters, in different ways. They may be confused by ambiguous, contradictory instructions, commands, and other behavioral cues. In any event, the constituent elements of organizations have interests of their own. All sorts of unexpected things therefore happen constantly inside organizations. To be sure, since everyone inside the system is under systemic constraints of some kind, the extent of unpredictability inside each system is lower than is the unpredictability of the external environment without a buffering organization to cushion its impacts. Nevertheless, because the expectations of regularity and dependability inside are high, even lesser disturbances arouse deep anxieties.

The leaders of organizations respond by trying to increase their control over actual and potential internal sources of irregularity just as they respond to external sources of uncertainty: they move from accommodation toward control. Irregularities of behavior alarm them because they seem to menace the processes of organization that must continue steadily if the organization is to survive. The leaders are also pushed by colleagues and coordinate units who complain to the leadership and demand action to curb or prod (as the case may be) their errant counterparts. The result of all this is the ubiquitous impulse toward centralization.

From the point of view of the leaders of *sub*organizations, the efforts of the leaders of the more inclusive organization constitute sources of uncertainty. Curiously enough, this is true even when the inclusive organization is *created by* previously autonomous smaller organizations seeking a way out of the uncertainties of competitive relations among them; as soon as they establish the overarching system, they find that it generates its own uncertainties as well as reducing others. So they begin to move to control it as well as each other. Occasionally, unable to acquire control, they try to withdraw from the system altogether. In one way or another, they react against uncertainty.

Such attempts to reduce uncertainty thus make all leaders, regardless of their personal inclinations, look power-hungry. They struggle for control over their subordinates. They try to manipulate their superiors, or to get away from them, and they try also to prevent their subordinates from doing the same to them. And they tend to struggle over boundaries with their coequals, whether the boundaries be territorial or functional.

Perhaps it *is* hunger for power that drives them, or quest for gain. Indeed, perhaps the differences between the appetites for power and gain on the one hand and aversion to unpredictability on the other are purely semantic. I emphasize the aversion to unpredictability because it seems to me to account for as many aspects of organizational behavior as the other hypothesized driving forces can explain, plus one additional characteristic: the seeming insatiability of whatever the driving force is. If it is simply the desire for power or gain, then the endless struggles within and among organizations can be explained only as products of limitless appetites that can never be satisfied no matter how much they acquire of

84

whatever is being sought. Aversion to unpredictability requires no such extraordinary assumption. Every measure to reduce uncertainties of one kind tends to foster uncertainties of another kind. Even in foodgetting, for example, intensive cultivation depleted soils and upset natural balances. Steps taken to diminish social uncertainties within and around organizations correspondingly engender fresh problems and threats. It is not necessary, then, to postulate a boundless hunger for power or material gain to make sense of the never-ending combat within and between organizations. Given the unavoidability of uncertainty, even a mild aversion to unpredictability is enough to explain these organizational impulses. That is why I focus on it rather than on other drives as the primary moving force in organizational life.

CONSEQUENCES OF THE AVERSION

The point of this excursus, to return to the main line of argument, is that if there is truly an aversion to unpredictability on the part of organizations, then the adoption of proposed changes will evoke all the mechanisms at the disposal of the organizations for maintaining or restoring predictability. Over and above the inclinations to reject *proposals* for change, reviewed in the first chapter, the *introduction* of change results in widespread efforts to isolate it, contain it, routinize it. For virtually all changes have unanticipated consequences and unintended effects. In the intricate network of relationships making up an organization, these unexpected results trace out their patterns in surprising ways. As soon as changes go into force, therefore, they become sources of uncertainty in many different parts of the system. And here and there, all through the system, the repertory of responses to uncertainty commences. Thus, instituting new practices or procedures or policies or programs in an organization is usually followed by strong counter-measures.

What is more, the countermeasures are not taken only by organization members immediately and adversely affected by the reforms. Even people seemingly remote from them, people whose stakes in the matters at issue are almost negligible, support steps to channel the disturbing new elements into regular, familiar patterns. For even at a distance, the unpredictable, with its possibilities for unforeseen fallout and spillover, heightens concern based on "abhorrence" of uncertainty.

Within a relatively short time, therefore, the spontaneity and exuberance of innovations are either completely absorbed into the old, ongoing activities of organizations by the combination of diverse forces bent on reducing uncertainty or they become the new, established, regularized practices. The aversion to unpredictability forges alliances of unlikely and even unrelated groups against potential distant threats as well as imminent dangers. The tolerances for uncertainty are narrow indeed.

THE ENVIRONMENTAL VESSEL

The architecture and procedures and policies of organizations are determined in large part by each organization's setting. Indeed, this relationship is precisely what is described by the term "adaptation." An organization adapts largely by fitting itself to its surroundings.

As we have seen, the surrounding also responds to the behavior of organizations. Even if an organization does not establish full control over its environment, elements of the environment adjust to what it does. So it would not be correct to portray organizations as purely passive, reactive creatures of the forces around them; they also shape the world they live in.

All the same, there is no question that many factors affecting organizational design and operation lie beyond the capacity of the leaders and members of the organization to alter them, at least in the short run. Every organization must come to terms with these if it is to survive.

Many of these factors, of course, are attributes of the physical and biological worlds. Although mankind has learned to manipulate many of them, to take advantage of them or to counterbalance and overcome them, it cannot escape or alter them fundamentally. In the social world as well, there are factors beyond the power of any given organization or group of organizations to modify substantially in the absence of nearly unanimous agreement among all organizations and peoples everywhere. After all, a species that universally condemns but cannot abolish war is obviously up against currently unmanageable forces—perhaps stupidity or ignorance, perhaps the selfishness of a few self-seeking and influential people, perhaps some deepseated and general psychological disorder, perhaps some defect in its institutions, but surely something not under its control—and clearly has many limitations on its ability to shape its environment and its destiny.

Whatever the limiting factors are, they oblige organizations to adjust to them. The most powerful organizations on earth are compelled to bow to this necessity. They may achieve remarkable successes in dominating some geographically or functionally adjacent sectors of their environments. If they reach out farther, they confront more intractable phenomena.

The intractability of the environment damps changes in organizations as soon as change occurs. In order to accomplish anything more extensive than marginal modifications, innovators usually discover they have to alter processes and policies far beyond the specific area with which they are directly concerned. The bigger or more fundamental the specific change they desire, the greater the distance they must go to effect it.

For example, when certain colleges decided to take affirmative action to increase the percentage of blacks and other minority groups in their student bodies, they found that it was not merely a matter of redefining admissions standards. Able students had to be sought out, but admissions officers had little relevant experience in searching for them after years of choosing among eager applicants who needed no prodding or encouragement to request admission. Their alumni, having come from a previously restricted segment of the population, could not pilot them into the minority populations of their own communities. Guidance counsellors in the high schools, governed by years of habit, if not by local prejudice and personal insecurity, discouraged members of minority groups from applying to nationally renowned institutions, and the students therefore seldom aspired to them. Segregated high schools in all parts of the country, starved for funds, were found to be graduating very few students who could meet the academic demands of good colleges. Moreover, the students' neighborhood environments, the poverty that forced them to earn money early, the obvious absence of opportunity for advancement in the larger community, and scores of other social factors furnished them with neither incentives nor opportunities to do well, and provided no stimulation or support for those who might have been so motivated.

If colleges took in poorly qualified students simply to demonstrate good will and commitment, they created problems on the campuses for both the minority students (who, above all, resented the condescension, both explicit and implied) and the faculties, and therefore for administrators. Meanwhile, the colleges with predominantly black student bodies, having been established because there was no other avenue to higher learning for most black young people and struggling to achieve academic excellence, were unable to compete for the best students and faculty members even though the need for these institutions continued.

The list of complications can be extended, but there is no need to labor the argument. What the colleges could change by manipulating formal requirements within their power would not come to much without very considerable changes in child-rearing practices and in precollege schooling and advising, in the structure of the job market for members of disadvantaged minorities, and in many of the internal practices of the colleges themselves. Unquestionably, many of these changes have been taking place. But bringing the proportion of blacks and other minorities in the college population up to something like their proportion in the total population is taking far longer than many advocates of equal educational opportunity had originally hoped or anticipated. The number of things that have to be modified to bring about such a change has turned out to be larger than they at first supposed.

Thus, the speed and extent of change are often curbed by the interdependence of organization and environment. That is one of the reasons why "tearing down" social institutions in order to rebuild them along radically different lines frequently disappoints the innovators. Not everything can be changed at once, even by a majority who desire to do so. As new institutions are built, they are compelled to adapt themselves to many of the conditions that molded their predecessors. Consequently, they come out resembling their predecessors in many respects. To be sure, different individuals or groups may be better off in the new system than they were in the old, and it is possible that *most* of the members may be better off, even though some are much worse off; I do not contend that organizational change makes no difference at all! I do believe, however, that every organization is so locked into its environment, and so many elements of the environment must be treated as parameters of change, that the overall patterns of their successors will be much like their own, even if they are entirely uprooted. In this sense, at least, the environment of an organization curbs the scope of change it can accomplish.

ORGANIZATIONS AS DAMPED SYSTEMS

For all these reasons, when change is introduced into a system, it usually does not set in motion a process of incessant, possibly explosive, oscillation. Such oscillations are possible. Innovators may put into effect changes that provoke stringent repressive reactions. To accomplish change in the face of repression generally requires a more forceful effort on the part of the innovators. This can call forth still harsher repressive measures. In this fashion, organizations can be pushed to the point of self-destructive internal warfare.

In most organizations, however, things do not come to such a pass. In the first place, the extremity of change is usually limited by the factors reviewed in this chapter. In the second place, those factors quickly stabilize and regularize the system so that most innovations are incorporated without alarming most members. The constrictions generated by the very strategies of the sponsors of change, the organizational aversion to unpredictability, and the complexities of the environment ordinarily damp the effects of change, so that the repercussions of innovation are progressively diminished.

To return to the question that was the point of departure for this book, it seems that if organizations die because they cannot adapt to a fluid environment it is because they are restrained by strong forces that keep them the way they are; although they are not as absolutely bound by these forces as an organism is by its genetic heritage, they are certainly not capable of altering themselves freely. What is more, when they employ strategies for effecting changes, the damping factors reviewed in this chapter keep the changes within bounds, or at least ensure that the innovations will soon become routine. I stress again that I am not asserting that inability to change is the only or even the chief cause of organizational death; I merely observe that it seems to be one of the causes. What I have tried to do so far is to account for failure to change in spite of what seems on the surface to be an unfettered potentiality to learn and adapt.

The attempt to explain these aspects of organizational life and death illuminates many other features and tendencies of organizational behavior; a number of implications flow from these premises. Exploring these implications is the object of the next chapter.

CHAPTER 4

SOME THEORETICAL IMPLICATIONS OF THE ARGUMENT

IN THE PRECEDING CHAPTERS, I tried to offer a personal, impressionistic synthesis of what has been observed, said, written, and demonstrated about organizational change, and I have suggested some explanations of the organizational behavior described. If the descriptions are faithful and the explanations valid, then a number of conclusions about the world of organizations may be drawn from them.

Ideally, the conclusions would be empirical statements deduced in strictly logical fashion from the preceding premises, and the accuracy or inaccuracy of the inferences would bolster confidence in or refute the argument. Unfortunately, not many of the inferences are sufficiently precise to permit the kind of measurement implicit in this scientific paradigm. And even the few that are this precise have not yet actually been subjected to careful and exact analysis. In that regard, I cannot even pretend to approach the scientific ideal.

What follows, therefore, is largely a logical exercise. I think it is a useful one, for if most of the assertions made in the previous pages are true, and if my reasoning in this chapter is not grossly in error, they compel some conclusions that are at least interesting and a few that I find surprising. Perhaps going off the deep end in this way will inspire (or provoke!) the sort of rigorous investigation that may improve the formulation offered here or, in the course of proving it false, contribute to the improvement of some other.

LITTLE BY LITTLE

There are people who apparently believe that the only way to accomplish systemic change is by totally destroying an existing system and constructing a new one. They are answered by defenders of gradual change, who see the dangers and costs of uprooting ongoing institutions as excessive. The rejoinder of the advocates of massive change is that doing things little by little is too slow and, anyway, merely refurbishes the old instead of building something new. The two views are almost never reconciled.

In point of fact, the differences are as much rhetorical as substantive. No one really believes that *everything* about a system can be changed all at once or even over a short time. Nor does anyone really believe that irritations, discontents, and injustices must be quietly endured indefinitely by the disadvantaged victims of systemic defects. Therefore, advocates of drastic and sweeping changes ordinarily tolerate continuation of many established practices, focusing only on selected ones which they consider to be especially important. Correspondingly, the guardians of tradition can accept all kinds of modifications if these do not threaten the particular continuities having special importance for them. For this reason, each group

93

can make some concessions to the other without yielding on any matters of fundamental principle, and thus they manage to live with each other (though not without tension and turbulence) in spite of the issues that divide them.

Because the definitions of revolution as against evolution are so largely matters of perspective, it is difficult to sort out the issues. Most people would probably agree on the relevant *dimensions* of change: the number of organizational attributes altered, the importance of those attributes, the extent of the alterations, and the period of time in which the alterations are completed probably describe the common distinctions between the terms. Fewer would agree on how to count attributes, on the measurement of the importance or the extent of change, or on the appropriate unit of time in individual cases. Consequently, what is massive and sudden to one observer will be called infinitesimal and glacial by another. Changes in race relations in the United States illustrate the point.

If we take a generation—twenty-five or thirty years, say—as a time frame, however, the factors reviewed in the preceding chapters almost ensure that any large organization will at the end of the interval be considered in all important respects more like what it was at the beginning than different from what it was at the beginning. There will be exceptions, of course, and many ambiguities. But in most cases, the continuities will be dominant and will include most of the distinguishing characteristics of each organization.

This stability is not a result of conscious choice or preference, although many people do like it. Rather, like biological change, it is an outcome of the way the world is ordered. The built-in tendencies of organizations not to change, and the dampers that come into play when change is nevertheless introduced, keep the number, magnitude, and importance of changes within rather narrow limits over any comparatively short period, such as a human generation. Perhaps it will be possible some day to redesign the whole dynamics of the biological and organizational worlds. Short of that (and we are still far short of it), we may learn to offset some of the damping factors but we apparently cannot eliminate them.

That is why, within this time horizon, organizational change takes place and will continue to take place by the accretion of small modifications of existing, ongoing systems. The process is not a result of a deliberately selected policy but, if the foregoing argument is correct, a characteristic of the organizational world just as it is of the biological world.

Controversy over changes will not always be proportionate to their magnitude or number or speed. People may attach great importance to modifications of modest scope compared to the scale of the whole enterprise on which they are worked; they may develop passionate loyalties to symbols, including purely arbitrary symbols like the names of telephone exchanges. And they may fight fiercely over these changes, small as the changes are by any objective index of extent. Thus, to say that organizational change normally occurs little by little is not to say it is accomplished harmoniously and easily.

It is not my intention to ridicule such concern for apparently limited changes. On the contrary, if the accumulation of limited changes is the way most large changes are accomplished, then concern for small ones, and a willingness to fight for them, can be essential for organizational adaptation. Anyway, it would be most presumptuous for any person to deride the values of others because they are attached to relatively small things—especially since each of us has his own values of this kind.

Rather, my purpose is to indicate the bearing of these inferences on the revolution-evolution discussion as it applies to organizational change. Try as we will, declaim as we may, most change in large organizations will be decidedly limited over the span of any human generation, and it is only by a steady accumulation of changes over longer periods that truly extensive transformations will take place.

ORGANIZATIONAL TURNOVER

Because organizations change only little by little, their survival rate should be closely associated with the rate of change in their environment. That is, if the environment also changes slowly, they should have no trouble adapting in spite of their own gradual pace of change. If the environment changes swiftly or unexpectedly, one would anticipate a fearful slaughter of organizations.

We are all prone to say that the world changes with blinding speed, even in the course of a single human lifetime. Obviously, the assertion is full of ambiguities, but it makes intuitive sense. Therefore, we may expect a very high death rate among organizations solely from failure to adapt. As we have seen, the fragmentary evidence at our disposal indicates that the organizational death rate is indeed great, and that failure to adapt is one of the plausible putative causes. The pieces seem to fit together, empirically as well as logically.

Yet if we examine the survival rate, we have a hard

time explaining why so many organizations presumably afflicted with rigidity manage to continue as *long* as they do in such a fluid environment. Without more reliable information about the organizational population and about environmental change, we can engage only in guesswork. But it is conceivable that large numbers of organizations live on for long periods in spite of the restraints on their ability to change themselves and their ways because the envirnoment is far *less* shifting and hostile than prevailing belief holds. That is, in the course of a human generation, the environment may make only modest demands on organizations, to which only the weakest ones are incapable of adjusting.

Deductive reasoning from the premises of the earlier chapters can thus lead in either of two diametrically opposed directions, and the choice must be regarded as an open one until we have better data than we have now. Only one thing is clear: whether the environment is stable or changing, benign or hostile, turnover among organizations will go on.

The death of any organization is usually accompanied by pain for at least some of the people associated with it. The compassionate desire to minimize such suffering induces some students to seek to reduce organizational mortality. Others consider organizational death and birth inefficient and wasteful ways of effecting innovations. So they seek ways to reduce mortality by increasing innovativeness.[1]

Not only is it unlikely, for reasons we have seen, that organizational mortality will ever be eliminated; it is also distinctly possible that the costs of overcoming the obstacles to change in ongoing organizations are higher than the costs of organizational death and replacement by new and different organizations. It may be more economical to introduce some innovations by replacing organizations than by reforming them. In fact, the death of intransigent or rigid but influential organizations may facilitate social change more readily than marginal adjustments that keep the old organizations alive but resistant to innovation. Turnover is thus not only unavoidable but possibly salutary.

ORGANIZATIONAL AGE

Whether turnover is high or low, whether the environment is benign or menacing, and no matter what the distribution of turnover by organizational age classes, we can expect to find a range of ages in any large organizational population, including some organizations that survive for extremely long periods (compared to human life spans) in spite of all the presumed obstacles to such longevity. These long-lived cases lend some credence to the hypothesis that organizations do not have species-limited life spans like most organisms.

Nevertheless, we are so accustomed to projecting onto organizations the properties of organisms (indeed, of people) that we ascribe to them attributes they may not have. I dare say, for example, that most of us would agree intuitively with the proposition that organizations grow more rigid as they grow older, just as most organisms do; and with the statement that as organizations grow older, their remaining life expectancy declines. Yet if we proceed from the argument in the preceding chapters, we come to just the opposite conclusion. By and large, the argument implies that the longer an organization survives, the more flexible it ought to be. And the longer it has already lived, the longer it is likely to persist into the future.

AGE AND FLEXIBILITY

Even if the environment of an organization changes gradually (in the time frame of a human generation), a very old organization must have overcome many change inhibitors to have lasted so long. The only exception would be an organization that has found an ecological niche in which the environment is almost invariant, making the total triumph of change inhibitors an asset rather than a liability. In all other cases, to have a long existence, with identity uninterrupted over generations, is proof of flexibility *cum* continuity. There is no *guarantee* that the secrets of success will be passed along from generation to generation in the organization, but one of the advantages of organizations over solitary individuals is that they do provide institutional memories longer than a human lifetime. Consequently, the chances are good that at least some of the advantages of experience will be passed along. Hence, older organizations ought logically to have acquired a broader repertory of adaptive skills than their younger counterparts.

I am not saying, "Older means wiser." Rather, I am denying that, when we speak of organizations, greater age automatically means more rigidity and less ability to change. On the contrary, if we could measure flexibility in some way, it might well turn out to be *positively* correlated with age. In this respect, the logic of the preceding chapters challenges common belief and organismic metaphors.

AGE AND LIFE EXPECTANCY

In like fashion, the logic of the preceding chapters suggests that the expectancy of life remaining to any organization ought to be positively correlated with the organization's age.[2] After all, if an organization is sufficiently traditional to maintain its continuing identity through generation after generation, yet sufficiently flexible to get past all the dangers from environmental changes along the way, it must either have been created with a very successful adaptive mechanism or have acquired one. If the mechanism served so well through so many environmental vicissitudes in the past, there is no self-evident reason why that honing and refining should not permit it to work well in response to the hazards and demands of the future. There is no *assurance* that it will; ancient organizations, like ancient biological species, can and doubtless do disappear. Logically, however, from the foregoing premises, the odds appear to run with age. This deduced hypothesis recognizes the organizational capacity for learning even if that capacity yields a good deal less flexibility (as a result of change inhibitors) than the word *learning* ordinarily connotes.

We are so accustomed to thinking of life in organismic terms, as a more or less fixed quantity irretrievably and irreplaceably depleted as it is consumed, that the idea of life as a growing balance instead of a declining one in the future of aging organizations contradicts one of our firm reference points. (Not even a breeder nuclear reactor, which produces fuel as it consumes fuel, is in the same category, superficially tempting as that analogy is.) Indeed, it appears that older biological species, let alone individual organisms, enjoy no such advantage over younger ones; previous and future longevity seem unrelated for them. In the world of living things, human organizations would thus be highly unusual if they do in fact exhibit this trait. Yet that is exactly what is implied by what precedes in this volume.

ORGANIZATIONAL SIZE

The logic of the argument offered here also raises questions about another popular belief, the assumption that organizations grow less capable of change as they increase in size. This belief finds support not only in common intuitions about large-scale bureaucracies and in common experience but even in the premises of my own argument: many of the barriers to change surveyed earlier seem more prominent in large organizations than in small ones. The deliberate programming of behavior, the division of work into minute tasks promoting tunnel vision, the accumulations of official and unofficial constraints on behavior, and the multiplication of interorganizational agreements all appear to be of greater intensity in larger organizations. It would seem to follow, therefore, that the larger an organization grows, at least when it comes to exceed some optimum size, the more rigid it becomes.

But if we take account of *all* the premises of my argument, they seem on balance to point in precisely the other direction—that is, to indicate that flexibility (defined as the capacity to conceive of changes and as receptivity to innovations) is related directly to organizational size. In other words, as a general rule, the larger an organization is, the more flexible it is likely to be.

THE THRUST TOWARD BIGNESS

This is not to say that organizations deliberately seek to increase their size in order to augment their flexibility. Rather, bigness is often an outgrowth of the aversion to uncertainty, and the accompanying flexibility (to be discussed below) both attends and reinforces this type of adjustment.

Size here refers to the number of people within an organization's boundaries. I postulated in Chapter III a tendency on the part of organizations to move from accommodation toward control, and to continue moving in this direction on that continuum until stopped by other forces. Since much of the unpredictability stimulating this response originates in adjacent organizations,[3] the impulse to bring them under control (when obliteration is infeasible) leads to efforts ranging from an extreme of complete absorption to some kind of federal arrangement all the way to confederation or loose association. All of these entail extending organization boundaries so as to bring the source of uncertainty under the control of some kind of acceptable leadership. Absorption brings it under the existing leadership of one of the organizations involved. Federation, confederation, and loose association bring all the organizations involved under the control of a common leadership established for the purpose, the differences among the forms turning on how much manipulative authority is conferred on the common leadership (or is acquired by it) as compared to the power retained by the component organizations. In all cases, however, the end of the process is a more inclusive organization embracing the combined membership of all the participating organizations.

Thus, reducing unpredictability by such means gives rise to larger and larger organizations, often by adding a more inclusive organization to the existing population.[4] In the economic sphere, not even public policies designed to prevent such inclusive organizations (trusts and cartels, for example) from forming have succeeded in suppressing this drive. In one way or another, undeterred by hostile laws and by political boundaries, firms manage to find ways to act in concert as though they were parts of more inclusive organizations, whether or not the containing organization is visible. In the political sphere, every grouping of people under governing bodies has given rise to efforts to group their governments, from leagues of city-states to empires, from nation-states to regional associations of governments and to the United Nations. The irrepressible push in this direction has led some observers to remark on the universal pressure to raise the level of integration in organizations.[5] The underlying cause, it seems to me, is the organizational aversion to unpredictability.

Hence organizations tend to get bigger and bigger. But, contrary to popular belief, not necessarily at the cost of their flexibility.

Bigness and Flexibility

Size and experimentation. Big organizations, because they usually have more resources at their disposal, are better able than small ones to support experiments that open up new possibilities for them, and they are better able to take advantage of opportunities afforded them by the discoveries of others. Admittedly, as I noted in the first chapter, organizations can be big and rich and still have resource problems because of sunk costs. And organizations can be big without necessarily being rich. All in all, however, other things being equal, large organizations usually are in a better position to experiment than small ones, and chances are good that even big ones with resource problems experiment more than small, rich ones. To be sure, small organizations appear on the scene doing things that big ones have not thought of; a good deal of social experimentation apparently takes this form. But when it comes to a deliberate search for new ways of doing things and new things to do, there is reason to suspect the big ones are out in front.

In the first place, in large organizations resources that would otherwise go to long-standing participants can be diverted with impunity to experimentation because deprivations shared by many members reduce the burdens on each to tolerable proportions. Small organizations usually lack this means of gathering the wherewithal for experimentation because each participant bears such a heavy part of the load that he resists.

In the second place, large organizations can duplicate internally the kind of probing and testing represented by the birth and death of small organizations in the broader social context. That is, using various subsystems for the purpose, they can try several different ways of doing the same thing in order to see which ones succeed, then proceed with the most promising systems and methods and abandon the others. They can create a kind of interior marketplace or competitive arena for ideas in which a "natural" selection takes place, thus preparing themselves for all kinds of possible environmental shifts without knowing ahead of time which shifts are likely to occur or what response is likely to be most effective.

In the third place, although the complexity of large organizations increases the number and force of change inhibitors, it also exposes many different kinds of specialists to each other's ideas and perspectives and interests. This exposure virtually ensures a flow of fresh ways of formulating and attacking problems—more, certainly, than will occur in a small organization encompassing a narrower range of specialties and tasks. Both small and large organizations are beset by tendencies that freeze them into their ongoing patterns, but large organizations probably stand a better chance of being jarred out of their ruts by their own internal diversity.

In the fourth place, large organizations are normally better able to assemble a "critical mass" of specialists in vital areas who can spark each other to develop new approaches to familiar problems. Small organizations are seldom in a position to gather such a "faculty" of experts, so they have more trouble recruiting them. Their isolated experts lack the stimulus and challenge and support of a face-to-face group of fellow professionals.

For these reasons, if for no others, large organizations can develop more repertories of behavior than their small counterparts, and these repertories come in handy as environmental conditions alter. This is one way in which bigness and flexibility go together.

Bigness and individual options. Big organizations also tend to allow freer play for individual preferences and idiosyncrasies than small ones do. As we have seen, they hold out many more role images for members to aspire to, and they generally offer a wider range of real role choices to choose among. Their composition is more heterogeneous, which in the long run broadens their tolerance of, and receptivity to, the unconventional. All organized life, as we have seen, requires conformity, but the degree of conformity that large organizations can impose and the range of behavior over which they can exert influence are often more limited than the corresponding capacities of small organizations; variety is built into the large ones. Finally, the impersonality of large organizations, whatever its vexations, constitutes a triumph of what Talcott Parsons has called achievement norms as against ascriptive norms (that is, recognition for accomplishment and competence rather than status) and universalistic rather than particularistic norms.[6] The result is that accidents of birth are less imprisoning; doors are opened to many who would otherwise be prevented from impressing themselves upon the system and registering their interests on its decisions; the system is loosened a little. In all these ways, large organizations willy-nilly generate and consider many more alternative ways of organizing and acting than do small ones.

These differences do not spring from qualitative differences in the people who inhabit organizations of different size, although it is conceivable that some self-selective membership factor is at work. Rather, the dynamics of systems of different size produce these effects. In smaller organizations, for example, the fortitude and determination required to stand up against the consensus of a face-to-face group are exceptional; the hostility of close comrades is usually much harder to endure than the disapprobation of the majority in large, impersonal surroundings. Moreover, the deviant is more visible in the smaller setting; social pressures on him to conform are more continuous and intense. What is more, a single nonconformist might upset the whole routine of a small system, while a large system may be less concerned about his oddities because it is not similarly threatened; the importance of conformity in the former leads to greater efforts to keep people in line or weed them out.

Taken all together, these elements explain why the tyranny of the village is often more oppressive than the coldness of the metropolis. They also explain why large organizations are often more able and willing to change than small ones.

SIZE AND SURVIVAL

If flexibility contributes to survival, and big organizations enjoy flexibility, then the survival rate of large organizations ought to be higher than that of small ones.[7] If large organizations have a good survival rate, then most very old organizations ought to be large ones. These inferences dovetail with those on age, flexibility, and life expectancy. Whether or not they are empirically valid is hard to say on the basis of the data now available on the age, size, and population of organizations. Logically, the inferences are consistent.

The expectation that big organizations would have a more favorable survival rate derives not only from the foregoing assumptions about flexibility but also from the theoretical capacity of large systems to absorb shocks and come through. They can contract and retrench in times of environmental pressure because they can excise troublesome subsystems and still continue, a course of action that is seldom feasible for small systems. By temporarily transferring slack resources from one part of the system to ailing parts, they can sustain the ailing parts until conditions are more hospitable to them. By drawing a little on all parts of the system in good times, they can build substantial reserves to be used in emergencies without draining any of the parts of their strength. In all, as we have already observed, they are better cushioned against variation in the environment. Where small organizations succumb, large ones often find the means to survive.

Large ones do go under, of course. In fact, it is quite possible that there is a size beyond which flexibility and survival rates begin to decline—a point of diminishing returns. Many economists comment on diseconomies of scale and other afflictions of firms that have become too big. No one can deny the possibility. But there is no such logical implication in the premises of this study. From a strictly deductive point of view, bigness and a comparatively high probability of survival seem to go together most of the time.

GRADATIONAL TENDENCIES OF POWER IN ORGANIZATIONS

My argument also compels me to conclude that power in organizations tends to diffuse slowly—gradually to distribute itself more and more evenly among the components and, eventually, among the members—in the course of time. It never reaches completely equal distribution—that state of harmonious reciprocity envisioned by philosophical anarchists and to a lesser extent by economic models of perfect competition—because long before it approaches such an ideal, other forces redistribute it unevenly again. But the continuing, the unremitting, force (as opposed to discontinuous, discrete counterforces) engenders slow movement toward greater uniformity of power.

At the risk of being taken too literally, I suggest that the appropriate analogy is to the geological gradational forces on the land portions of the earth. Wind and water and other erosive factors tend to level out the surface, abrading mountains and filling in depressions, constantly smoothing out the land. From time to time, a cataclysmic event will heave up a chain of peaks or a volcanic cone, or leave a vast scar across the surface. The gradational forces go on grinding things smooth. They have never fully polished the surface (although it is said to be smoother than a bowling ball in relative terms), and will never do so unless the periods between upheavals lengthen enormously. If it were not for the upheavals, however, they would eventually succeed.

In roughly comparable fashion, many organizational change inhibitors owe their effect to the gradational tendencies of power. They consist in a capacity to block unwanted action—a capacity acquired, as we have seen, by more and more components of a system the longer the system exists without change. That is why innovation in such an organization demands great investments of energy. It is also why so many organizational upheavals transfer power to a central leadership; the need for action sometimes wins more support than the desire for participation.

The metaphor should not be pressed too far. Geological upheavals do not seem to occur in reaction to gradational forces, nor do the forces of gradation owe their existence to upheavals. In contrast, upheavals that concentrate power in organizations are triggered to a large extent by the effects of previous power diffusion, and demands to share power in turn are caused partly by reaction to upheavals. The geological and organizational processes are not at all the same. As a figure of speech, to clarify one element of the analysis, the analogy is useful only to illuminate the proposition that in the absence of occasional episodes of centralization, power in organizations gravitates downward. Or to put it another way, if you see an organization that has not undergone an upheaval in many years, the likelihood is that the power is more widely shared than it was originally. And the longer the organization goes without an upheaval, the more it is likely to continue to drift in the same direction. It does not follow that every organizational upheaval centralizes power, or that every period of relative tranquility diffuses it. But if my interpretation is valid, then these will be the tendencies in most such instances.

ORGANIZATIONAL EVOLUTION

Is there, in all this, a secular trend toward some dominant organizational form? Are the lines of development proceeding step by step toward an all-inclusive, immortal, global form of organization? Do the lines of evolution converge on a single ultimate outcome?

Some observers have seemed to think so. Marx, for instance, presented a unilinear theory of historical development that would presumably end in a world-wide state of unchanging equilibrium and harmony once the warfare between classes was terminated by the triumph of the proletariat. More recently, a group of biologists and anthropologists foresaw the emergence of a universal "epiorganism" as the final stage in the rise of the level of integration that began its ascent when life moved from the single-celled through the multicellular form of biological organization to the development of social forms.[8] Still more recently, Roderick Seidenberg predicted the appearance of "post-historic man,"[9] who would be a prisoner of his unchanging organizations as prehistoric man was a prisoner of his unchanging "instincts."

Others see social evolution, like biological evolution, as multilinear,[10] fanning out in many directions at once, with the process of mutation and natural selection going on for as long as mankind and other forms of life endure. Continuing differentiation and diversification offset the disappearance of species selected out. The birth of new types at least balances out the death of the old.

From the premises presented in this volume, I must conclude that both forecasts are right. The views are not mutually exclusive, but complementary. Both unilinear and multilinear evolution take place simultaneously, and neither nullifies the other.

The analysis of organizational age and size, and the thrust toward more inclusive organizations, do indeed suggest development of huge systems encompassing more and more of the people in the world (though as members of subsystems rather than of the parent systems directly) and exercising influence over more and more functions. Each such creation will be a kind of upheaval, though not necessarily violent, increasing centralization in human affairs. The initial attempts will be hesitating and circumscribed, so even at their start these institutions will be weak; the gradational tendencies of power will weaken them further and some may even fall apart. But the forces that gave rise to them in the first place will generate new efforts, and as the leaders of the new system deal with the internal and external sources of uncertainty confronting them, they will produce additional centralizations of power from time to time. There is a secular trend toward global leadership institutions, and there is no reason to think, on the basis of any of the evidence now at hand, that it will be halted. Perhaps it will eventually reach an impasse, as George Orwell predicted in *1984*, with the process coming to an end as three massive systems achieve a state of perfect equilibrium among themselves. It seems to me more likely that the unpredictable elements in such a condition and the delicacy of the equipoise will lead inevitably to the final step, a global directorate of some sort. Indeed, it may be said that the growth and outward thrust of organizations have already established a single world-wide system, so that the next step is merely the development of a leadership group with world-wide perspectives and interests different from those of any of the current participants, and with resources for registering those viewpoints and concerns on the behavior of the system.

Such a comprehensive system will not mean uniformity or stasis. Within it, new forms will appear and old ones will give way; turnover will persist. Some of the new forms will be better suited to the conditions of their times and places than others, and will therefore multiply, in turn giving rise to new variants. In short, organizational evolution will continue for a long time, proceeding along many lines, just as it always has.

These tendencies do not portend a restful, carefree, harmonious world in the foreseeable future. Organizations will continue to change slowly, and the difference between their rate of change and the speed of changes in human aspirations and expectations will generate familiar tensions for many generations to come. Organizations will still be born in hope and optimism and go down in sadness and disappointment. Perhaps the rising level of integration will curtail some of the most egregious human follies; it is not unreasonable to hope so. But the main features of organizational behavior today will be recognizable to people in the near future, whatever happens.

Recognizing the factors that shape events has in the past been the prelude to mastering them. The Tolstoyan view of history, which portrays even the greatest of leaders as mere chips on the crest of historic tides they do not control, may prove too pessimistic; mankind may yet emerge as master of its own destiny. The deciphering of the genetic code and the astonishing development of computers in the last half of this century may constitute a threshold to a future that the ordinary mind cannot even imagine. Evolutionary processes that now function blindly, through chance, may be steered and directed.

If so, understanding the forces that now govern us will be more urgent than ever, for tinkering with the processes could have disastrous consequences. In any event, however, knowing the natural history of organizations will be increasingly important because large-scale organizations are here to stay as long as human culture survives; there will be no return to a world of simpler, smaller units. To preserve the values of a free society and of democratic life within these systems is a challenge of vast proportions. Perhaps it can never be met, but only if we broaden and deepen our insights into organizations will there be any chance at all that it can.

APPENDIX

ORGANIZATIONAL DEATH

THE PROBLEM

The concept of organizational death presents a trouble-some logical problem. As organizations learn what sorts of adaptations are required for survival, they may theoretically change themselves to satisfy those requirements. But how many changes can an organization make before it is regarded as a totally new organization? After all, there does come a point at which it makes no sense to consider the original system still in existence; the Tin Woodman in the Wizard of Oz notwithstanding, replacement of enough components eventually makes a new entity, and the old one must be pronounced dead, even though the process of replacement has been gradual. Since organizations generally do change gradually, at what point should it be said that the original organization no longer exists?

This is not exclusively an organizational dilemma; it is true of organisms as well. The criteria that used to suffice to define organismic death turned out to be less precise than medical authorities would have wished when organ transplantation from dead to living persons became possible. But the standard criteria do very well for most purposes; with rare exceptions, there is not much argument about whether an organism is alive or dead.

The reason is that the definition of organismic death centers on one or two discontinuities. If certain designated processes continue (say, heartbeat or electrochemical activity in the central nervous system), we consider the individual alive and the same person he always was, even though he may have doubled his weight, grown a beard, adopted a new trade, changed his name, taken a new wife, acquired a new language, migrated to a new country, experienced personality changes, and even lost his memory within the previous few years. By the same token, though he may have changed in none of these respects, the individual is pronounced dead when the specified biological processes are interrupted for comparatively brief periods of time. The ambiguities are really quite minimal.

Not so with organizations. We might have no trouble agreeing that a manufacturing company continues to exist even though it has changed its name, for example, but what if it has also changed its product? Its top officers? Its rank-and-file membership? Its clientele? Its location? Its structure? Its owners? Its creditors and debtors? Just how far would it have to go before everyone would agree that the original organization is "dead"? When is it no longer an ongoing organization but a new one replacing an older one that died?

ORGANIZATION BOUNDARIES AND LIFE

We have no definitive answer, and perhaps none is possible. As a tentative rule of thumb, however, the demarcation and defense of organizational boundaries might be useful as a key continuity. Since every organization has some way of distinguishing its inner components from its outer environment, might it not usefully be regarded as surviving as long as this distinction is maintained uninterrupted? Once the borders become indistinguishable for any length of time, all other indicia of collective life that constitute evidence of organizational existence will probably also have ceased. As long as the borders endure, the collectivity may be treated as an ongoing one in spite of most other changes in its character or activities.

Boundaries of organizations are usually marked by several methods, so the suggested index of continuous existence can be given operational content. For example, boundaries are commonly signalized by marks of membership, such as uniforms, badges, certificates, or inclusion on rosters; by rites of boundary crossing, such as induction ceremonies, award of symbols of membership, retirement parties, or expulsion rituals; by evidences of organizational jurisdiction, such as the distribution of the burdens and benefits of membership; and by the perimeters of communications networks, as outlined, for instance, by eligibility for official, internal communiqués. If none of these practices were conducted regularly in a group, then the group would not ordinarily be thought to possess any of the properties of an organization, and any organization that had ceased to conduct them could meaningfully be said to have died.

ORGANIZATIONAL BONDS

When the boundaries of an organization can no longer be distinguished, it is safe to assume that the bonds holding the organization together have dissolved. The "magnetism" that binds members of organizations to each other includes: (1) emotional bonds (probably the strongest ones) —love (of all by each, of a common leader, a common symbol, and/or a common idea), hate or fear (of all alternatives to membership); (2) moral bonds— the feeling one *ought* to belong and obey and conform; (3) bonds of expediency—rational calculation of the benefits and costs of membership in a given association as against membership in a different one or in none at all; (4) habitual bonds; (5) physical bonds—prison walls, the coastline of an island, the surface of a planet. The greater the number of bonds holding an organization together, the harder it is to disintegrate it and the more likely it is to reassemble itself after having been forcibly dismantled. Indeed, an association united by all five kinds of bonds can probably be extinguished only by killing all its members; brutal terror and overwhelming force may disrupt it for a time, but they cannot wipe it out. Such an organization has remarkable internal strength.

Most organizations, however, are not united by such a variety of bonds. In modern societies, in fact, expediential bonds are probably the most extensively employed type. (That is why so much organization theory is addressed almost exclusively to the rational calculation of inducements to enter and contribute to an organization.) The presence of even a few weak bonds may therefore be taken to indicate the existence of an organization.

Theoretically, the bonds themselves would constitute an excellent index of organizational existence and vitality. But they are even more difficult to define, detect, and measure than boundaries. For this reason, the boundaries are probably the more reliable index, even though they convey a minimum of information about the state of an organization.

WORKING WITH THE INDEFINABLE

All discussions of organization theory thus have an elusive character. We are hard put to define the subject; March and Simon wrote an outstanding book on it, yet eschewed definition.[1] And we cannot even say confidently whether our specimens are alive or dead.

It is possible we are pursuing a will-o'-the-wisp. It is also possible that our difficulties of definition are not fatal flaws at this stage of theoretical development. All categories grow hazy at the borders, even seemingly precise ones. We need to sharpen our concepts and our measuring instruments. We should not, however, refrain from grappling with the study of organizations simply because our tools for doing so are still crude. As March and Simon contend, we can give examples of organizational birth, existence, and death. For the time being, that may be enough.

NOTES

CHAPTER 1

1. C. I. Barnard, *The Functions of the Executive* (Cambridge, Mass.: Harvard University Press, 1938), p. 5.

2. Dun & Bradstreet, Inc., *The Failure Record through 1969* (New York: Dun & Bradstreet Inc., 1970), p. 2; E. D. Hollander, *et al.*, *The Future of Small Business* (New York: Frederick A. Praeger, 1967), pp. 222–23.

3. It should be noted that the acknowledged collective benefits of stability are as important to proponents of change as they are to defenders of tradition. Innovations would hardly be worth working for if there were not a presumption that they would persist for a long time after their adoption; why pour effort into bringing about changes that are likely to be supplanted or even reversed in short order? To know that changes, once made, will be favored by the logic of organized life is reassuring to the advocates of these changes in spite of the fact that the logic works against them while they are insurgents. And because the changes *are* so favored when they prevail, the trimuphant innovators soon begin to sound like the reactionaries they previously denounced.

4. The almost universal tendency of people to forget favors and remember slights or injuries constitutes Kaufman's Law: "What sticks in your craw sticks in your mind."

5. See H. Kaufman, *The Forest Ranger* (Baltimore: Johns Hopkins Press, 1960), chapter 6; O. G. Stahl, *Public Personnel Administration* (New York: Harper & Brothers, 4th ed., 1956).

6. A. Huxley, *Brave New World* (New York: The Modern Library, 1956); G. Orwell, *1984* (New York: Signet Books, 1950); W. H. Whyte, Jr., *The Organization Man* (New York: Doubleday & Co., 1957).

7. T. Parsons and E. A. Shils, eds., *Toward a General Theory of Action* (New York: Harper & Row, 1962), pp. 76–91.

8. See, for example, H. C. Mansfield and F. Marx Morstein, "Informal Organization," in Morstein Marx, ed., *Elements of Public Administration* (Englewood Cliffs: Prentice-Hall, 1949), 2nd ed., pp. 274–93; P. R. Lawrence, *et al.*, *Organizational Behavior and Administration* (Homewood, Ill.: The Dorsey Press & Richard D. Irwin, 1961), especially sections II, V, and VII; P. M. Blau and W. R. Scott, *Formal Organizations* (San Francisco: Chandler Publishing Co., 1962), pp. 89–100, 234–37.

CHAPTER 2

1. H. A. Simon, D. W. Smithburg, and V. A. Thompson, *Public Administration* (New York: Alfred A. Knopf, 1950), chapter 7.

2. See R. B. Zajonc, "Conformity," in *International Encyclopedia of the Social Sciences* (New York: The Macmillan Company & The Free Press, 1968).

3. Simon, Smithburg, and Thompson, *Public Administration,* chapters 21 and 22.

CHAPTER 3

1. This section is based on my "Why Organizations Behave as They Do: An Outline of a Theory," in *Papers Presented at an Interdisciplinary Seminar on Administrative Theory,*

jointly sponsored by the Department of Educational Administration, the Department of Management, and the Department
of Government, The University of Texas, March 20–21, 1961.

CHAPTER 4

1. See, for example, V. A. Thompson, *Bureaucracy and Innovation* (University, Ala.: University of Alabama Press,
1969), p. 4.

2. This conclusion was reached by Anthony Downs in his
Inside Bureaucracy (Boston: Little, Brown & Co., 1967), in
which he declares at page 20: "The older a bureau is, the less
likely it is to die."

3. I use *adjacent* in the functional sense (to refer to organizations whose outputs become direct inputs of a given organization or whose inputs include the direct output of a
given organization) as well as in the spatial sense.

4. I do not mean to imply that the aversion to unpredictability is the *only* reason for organizational growth, or that
growth takes place *only* by fusion of existing organizations.
On the contrary, there are many reasons for organizations to
grow; see, for example, W. H. Starbuck, "Organizational
Growth and Development," in J. G. March, ed., *Handbook
of Organizations* (Chicago: Rand McNally & Co., 1965), pp.
453–67. And the accretion of members by recruitment and/or
natural increase also enlarges organizations. I suggest only that
uncertainty reduction is a very prominent yet often neglected
impulse toward growth, and that it is particularly important
in growth by fusion. Moreover, this thrust toward growth continues as long as there are any external sources of unpredictability impinging on an organization, so that it is almost universal and will take effect unless counteracted by other forces;
as in the case of a ball blocked from rolling down an inclined
plane, the impulse is always in the same direction.

5. See R. Redfield, ed., *Levels of Integration in Biological and Social Systems* (Lancaster, Pa.: Jaques Cattell Press, 1942) ; Simon, Smithburg, and Thompson, *Public Administration,* p. 272.

6. T. Parsons and E. A. Shils, eds., *Toward a General Theory of Action,* pp. 82–83.

7. Starbuck, pp. 463–64. See also the discussion of the "urban size ratchet" in W. R. Thompson, *A Preface to Urban Economics* (Baltimore: The Johns Hopkins Press, 1965) , pp. 21–24.

8. Redfield, *Levels of Integration in Biological and Social Systems.*

9. R. Seidenberg, *Post-Historic Man* (Boston: The Beacon Press, 1957) .

10. J. H. Steward, *Theory of Culture Change: The Methodology of Multilinear Evolution* (Urbana: University of Illinois Press, 1955) ; ———, "Evolution and Process," in Kroeber, A. L., ed., *Anthropology Today* (Chicago: The University of Chicago Press, 1953) , pp. 313–26.

APPENDIX

1. J. G. March and H. A. Simon, *Organizations* (New York: John Wiley & Sons, Inc., 1958) . In their very first paragraph, the authors declare: "It is easier, and probably more useful, to give examples of formal organizations than to define the term. . . . [F]or present purposes, we need not trouble ourselves about the precise boundaries to be drawn around an organization or the exact distinction between an 'organization' and a 'nonorganization.' We are dealing with empirical phenomena, and the world has an uncomfortable way of not permitting itself to be fitted into clean classifications."

INDEX